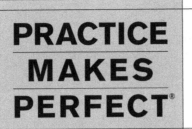

**PRACTICE
MAKES
PERFECT**

Fractions, Decimals, AND Percents

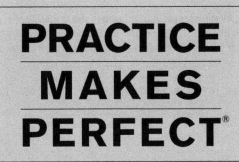

PRACTICE MAKES PERFECT®

Fractions, Decimals, AND Percents

Erin Muschla-Berry

New York   Chicago   San Francisco   Lisbon   London   Madrid   Mexico City
Milan   New Delhi   San Juan   Seoul   Singapore   Sydney   Toronto

ISBN   978-0-07-177286-0
MHID   0-07-177286-3

e-ISBN   978-0-07-178122-0
e-MHID   0-07-178122-6

Library of Congress Control Number 2012931069

Contents

About this book

Three math topics that students often fear are fractions, decimals, and percents. These topics can bring panic to even the most capable math students. *Practice Makes Perfect: Fractions, Decimals, and Percents* is a valuable resource that can help students master the concepts and skills necessary for understanding these topics. The book contains 45 lessons and 83 exercises of practice problems.

Students, their parents, and teachers will find this book useful. Students may work independently or with their parents on the concepts and skills presented in this book. They may use the material for extra practice or enrichment. Teachers may supplement their lessons and activities with the examples and practice problems.

Fractions, decimals, and percents include a wide range of concepts and skills that are fundamental to mathematical understanding. Mastery of these topics provides a strong foundation for success in future math courses.

How to use this book

Practice Makes Perfect: Fractions, Decimals, and Percents is divided into six sections. Each section includes several lessons with detailed explanations, examples, and exercises containing practice problems. An answer key is provided at the end of the book.

Chapter 1, "Understanding fractional relationships," presents basic skills and terminology associated with fractions. This section includes 10 lessons and 18 exercises that focus on modeling fractions, least common multiples, greatest common factors, comparing fractions, ordering fractions, converting fractions to mixed numbers and mixed numbers to fractions, and simplifying fractions.

Chapter 2, "Operations with fractions," includes 12 lessons and 22 exercises. This section focuses on addition, subtraction, multiplication, and division of fractions and mixed numbers.

Chapter 3, "Connecting fractions and decimals," shows the relationship between fractions and decimals. It includes 8 lessons and 12 exercises that focus on place value, converting fractions to decimals and decimals to fractions, as well as the basic skills associated with decimals.

Chapter 4, "Operations with decimals," includes 5 lessons and 10 exercises. This section focuses on adding, subtracting, multiplying, and dividing decimals.

Chapter 5, "Connecting fractions, decimals, and percents," shows the relationships among fractions, decimals, and percents. It includes 4 lessons and 8 exercises. In addition, it focuses on the basic terminology associated with percents.

Chapter 6, "Operations with percents," contains percent problems such as finding the percent of a number, finding what percent one number is of another, finding the percent when a number is known, markups, markdowns, sales tax, percent of change, and computing simple interest. This section contains 6 lessons and 13 exercises.

Each lesson begins with an explanation of a concept or skill and contains examples and step-by-step instructions for solving problems. Most lessons are followed by two exercises of practice problems, with the first being self-correcting. Each self-correcting exercise contains easy-to-follow directions and requires no additional materials. By finishing the exercise, you will be able to complete a statement and discover an interesting fact.

To get the most from this book, always read the explanation of a lesson and study the examples before beginning an exercise. If you need help once you start an exercise, refer back to the lesson and examples. When you are done, be sure to check your answers with the answer key. For any problems in which you made a mistake, double-check your work. Finding, understanding, and correcting mistakes is the key to mastering concepts and skills.

The exercises and practice problems in this book provide a vast amount of material that will help you to learn and master fractions, decimals, and percents. With hard work and practice, you will gain the knowledge necessary for success in mathematics.

Understanding fractional relationships

What is a fraction?

Fractions represent a part of a whole. For example, the square shown here represents 1 whole because it is one whole square.

If this square is divided into 4 equal squares as shown here, these 4 equal parts are equivalent to 1 whole.

In the figure that follows, 1 of the 4 squares is shaded. This can be written as the fraction $\frac{1}{4}$. The numerator, or the top number of a fraction, represents the number of parts that are shaded. The denominator, or the bottom number of a fraction, represents the number of equal parts that make 1 whole.

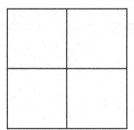

In the next figure, there are two large squares. In the first, 2 of the 4 small squares are shaded. This can be written as the fraction $\frac{2}{4}$. The numerator is 2 because two of the small squares are shaded. The denominator is 4 because 4 equal parts make 1 whole. The fraction $\frac{2}{4}$ can also be written as $\frac{1}{2}$. The fraction $\frac{1}{2}$ is seen in the second square. There is one shaded rectangle out of two total rectangles. Notice that in both squares, the shaded sections are equivalent, or represent the same amount. The two large squares show the same relationship. $\frac{2}{4}$ and $\frac{1}{2}$ are equivalent because they represent the same part of 1 whole.

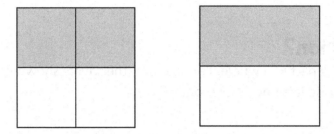

Example 1: Write a fraction for the model that follows.

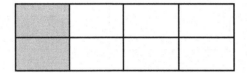

- In this figure, 8 equal parts make up 1 whole. 8 is the denominator. Because 2 equal parts are shaded, 2 is the numerator.

- The fraction that represents this model is $\frac{2}{8}$. This can also be expressed as $\frac{1}{4}$ because 1 of the 4 equal columns is shaded.

Example 2: Draw a model that represents $\frac{2}{3}$.

- When drawing a model you may select any shape to use. Make sure that the shape can easily be divided into equal parts.

- Decide how many equal parts represent 1 whole. In $\frac{2}{3}$, 3 is the denominator. 3 equal parts represent 1 whole figure.

- Decide how many equal parts should be shaded. 2 equal parts should be shaded because the numerator is 2.

Following is a model that represents $\frac{2}{3}$.

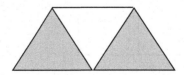

Write a fraction that describes each figure.

1.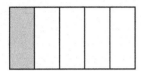

2.

3.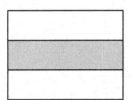

4.

5.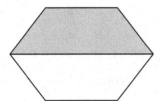

6.

7.

8.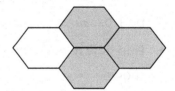

Draw a model that represents each fraction.

9. $\dfrac{3}{4}$

10. $\dfrac{5}{6}$

11. $\dfrac{6}{8}$

12. $\dfrac{2}{5}$

13. $\frac{7}{9}$

14. $\frac{3}{3}$

15. $\frac{1}{10}$

16. $\frac{1}{6}$

Fractions on a number line

Every fraction can be represented on a number line. Using number lines helps you understand the value of each fraction and its relation to other fractions and whole numbers.

Example 1: Place $\frac{3}{4}$ on a number line.

- ◆ Find how many equal parts make up 1 whole. This is shown by the denominator. The denominator in $\frac{3}{4}$ is 4. 4 equal parts represent 1 whole.

- ◆ Write the whole numbers 0 and 1 on your number line.

- ◆ Mark 3 evenly spaced lines, called tick marks, between 0 and 1. The fourth line should be 1 because 4 equal parts are the same as 1 whole.

- ◆ Find how many of those equal parts are shown in the fraction. In $\frac{3}{4}$, 3 equal parts are shown.

- ◆ Place a point on the line that represents $\frac{3}{4}$. This is the third line after zero because it represents 3 tick marks out of the 4 that make up 1 whole.

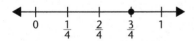

Example 2: Place $\frac{2}{3}$ and $\frac{5}{6}$ on the same number line.

- ◆ Find how many parts equal 1 whole. This problem has two fractions. In $\frac{2}{3}$, 3 equal parts represent 1 whole. In $\frac{5}{6}$, 6 equal parts represent 1 whole. Because 6 is the larger denominator, divide the number line into 6 equal parts.

- ◆ Write the whole numbers 0 and 1 on your number line.

- Mark 5 evenly spaced lines between 0 and 1. The sixth line represents 1 because 6 equal parts are the same as 1 whole.

- Place a point on $\frac{5}{6}$. This is represented by the fifth tick mark after zero.

- Find how many sixths are equal to $\frac{2}{3}$. You can divide the entire number line you drew into 3 equal parts. The mark for $\frac{1}{3}$ is the same as $\frac{2}{6}$, and the mark for $\frac{2}{3}$ is the same as $\frac{4}{6}$. Place a point on $\frac{4}{6}$ to show $\frac{2}{3}$.

- $\frac{2}{3}$ and $\frac{5}{6}$ are shown on the following number line.

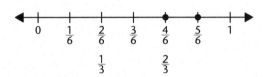

EXERCISE
1·2

Draw a number line for each fraction or pair of fractions.
Place the fractions on their number line.

1. $\frac{2}{5}$

2. $\frac{1}{6}$

3. $\frac{1}{2}$

4. $\frac{6}{7}$

5. $\frac{3}{10}$

6. $\frac{1}{3}$

7. $\frac{5}{8}$

8. $\frac{4}{9}$

9. $\dfrac{4}{10}$ and $\dfrac{7}{10}$

10. $\dfrac{2}{4}$ and $\dfrac{3}{8}$

11. $\dfrac{1}{3}$ and $\dfrac{5}{6}$

12. $\dfrac{4}{6}$ and $\dfrac{1}{2}$

13. $\dfrac{2}{3}$ and $\dfrac{3}{9}$

14. $\dfrac{4}{5}$ and $\dfrac{1}{10}$

15. $\dfrac{7}{12}$ and $\dfrac{2}{6}$

16. $\dfrac{8}{9}$ and $\dfrac{3}{3}$

Finding the least common multiple (LCM)

A multiple is the product of a number and a counting number. For example, the multiples of 3 are 3 × 1, 3 × 2, 3 × 3, 3 × 4, 3 × 5, . . . or 3, 6, 9, 12, 15, . . .

A common multiple of two numbers is a multiple that is shared by the two numbers. For example, the multiples of 3 are listed above. The multiples of 4 are 4, 8, 12, 16, 20, . . . The common multiples of 3 and 4 are the multiples that are common to both 3 and 4. If the lists of the multiples of 3 and 4 were extended, 12, 24, 36, . . . would be on both lists. They are some of the common multiples of 3 and 4. The least common multiple (LCM) of two numbers is the smallest number that is a common multiple of both numbers. The LCM of 3 and 4 is 12.

There are two methods for finding the LCM: making a list and using prime factorization.

Method 1: Make a list

Making a list can be an effective method when the numbers are small and their LCM is close to the beginning of the list you make. But if the LCM is large, or if you have large numbers, a list will be difficult to make.

Example: Find the LCM of 5 and 6.

◆ List the multiples of 5.

 5, 10, 15, 20, 25, 30, 35, 40, . . .

◆ List the multiples of 6.

 6, 12, 18, 24, 30, . . .

◆ Because 30 is the first number common to both lists, 30 is the LCM of 5 and 6.

Method 2: Use prime factorization

Prime factorization of a whole number is defined as writing the number as a product of its prime factors. A prime number has only two factors: 1 and the number itself. 2 is a prime number because its only factors are 1 and 2. 3 is a prime number because its only factors are 1 and 3. 2, 3, 5, 7, 11, 13, 17, and 19 are the prime numbers less than 20.

Composite numbers have more than two factors. 4 is a composite number because its factors are 1, 2, and 4. 6 is a composite number because its factors are 1, 2, 3, and 6. 4, 6, 8, 9, 10, 12, 14, 15, 16, and 18 are the composite numbers less than 20.

To use prime factorization to find the LCM, create a factor tree by writing one of the numbers that you are given at the top of the tree. Start with two factors of this number. It is helpful if one of these two factors is a prime number, but you can start with any two factors. Then factor the factors until the last number on each branch consists of only prime numbers. Follow the same procedure with the second number. Once you have found the prime factorization of both numbers, write the prime factorization using exponents to find the LCM.

Example: Find the LCM of 24 and 30

◆ Make a factor tree for each number. For 24, start with 2 and 12. (You can also start with 3 and 8 or 4 and 6.) For 30, start with 2 and 15. (You can also start with 3 and 10 or 5 and 6.)

◆ Since 12 and 15 are composite numbers, they must be factored. Factor 12 as 2 × 6. Factor 15 as 3 × 5.

◆ The factors of 30 are 2, 3, and 5, which are all prime numbers. The factor tree for 30 is now complete. The prime factorization of 30 is 2 × 3 × 5. The prime factorization for 24 is not complete, because 6 is a composite number. Continue making the factor tree by factoring 6 as 2 × 3.

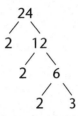

◆ The factor tree for 24 is now complete. The prime factorization of 24 is 2 × 2 × 2 × 3.

◆ Rewrite each prime factorization using exponents. The exponents tell how many times each prime number is used as a factor. (For example $2 × 2 × 2 = 2^3$.)

The prime factors of 24 = 2 × 2 × 2 × 3 or 2^3 × 3

The prime factors of 30 = 2 × 3 × 5.

Write each prime factor and only the largest exponent of each. 2^3 × 3 × 5

Find the product. 2^3 × 3 × 5 = 120

The LCM of 24 and 30 is 120.

EXERCISE

1·3

Find the LCM using the method given. Write the letter of the problem in the space above its answer at the end of the exercise to complete the sentence. Some answers will be used more than once. Some answers will not be used.

Make a list to find the LCM of each pair of numbers.

C.   5 and 9

N.   10 and 15

A. 9 and 6

R. 35 and 7

M. 5 and 20

O. 17 and 3

Use prime factorization to find the LCM of each pair of numbers.

I. 28 and 12

S. 36 and 8

E. 50 and 20

L. 6 and 42

U. 15 and 20

T. 72 and 12

The ___ ___ ___ ___ ___ ___ ___ ___ ___ ___ ___ ___ ___ ___ ___ ___
    144 35 18 30 72 45 51 30 144 84 30 100 30 144 18 42

Railroad was the first railroad to connect the east and west coasts of the United States. It was built in 1862.

Make a list to find the LCM of each pair of numbers.

1. 5 and 15

2. 3 and 8

3. 12 and 8

4. 14 and 6

5. 7 and 9

6. 10 and 8

7. 15 and 2

8. 6 and 9

Use prime factorization to find the LCM of each pair of numbers.

9. 14 and 30

10. 10 and 25

11. 12 and 15

12. 28 and 14

13. 18 and 20

14.   22 and 52

15.   24 and 36

16.   36 and 40

Equivalent fractions

Equivalent fractions are fractions that have the same value, although they have different numerators and different denominators. Equivalent fractions are modeled in the figures that follow. Notice that although the numerators and denominators are different in each fraction, they represent the same amount of the square on each model.

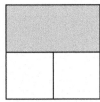
The shaded part of this square equals $\frac{1}{2}$.

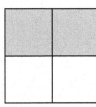
The shaded part of this square equals $\frac{2}{4}$.

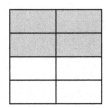
The shaded part of this square equals $\frac{4}{8}$.

To find equivalent fractions, multiply or divide the numerator and denominator by the same number.

Example 1: Write an equivalent fraction: $\frac{2}{3} = \frac{}{6}$.

◆   Because the denominator, 3, is multiplied by 2 to find 6, multiply the numerator, 2, by 2 to find 4. $\frac{2}{3} = \frac{2 \times 2}{3 \times 2} = \frac{4}{6}$

◆ $\frac{2}{3}$ is equivalent to $\frac{4}{6}$.

Example 2: Find if $\frac{3}{4}$ *is equivalent to* $\frac{9}{12}$.

◆   You can also find equivalent fractions by using division. Because both the numerator, 9, and the denominator, 12, can be divided by 3 to equal $\frac{3}{4}$, these fractions are equivalent. $\frac{9}{12} = \frac{9 \div 3}{12 \div 3} = \frac{3}{4}$

Find equivalent fractions. Write the letter of the problem in the space above its answer at the end of the exercise to complete the sentence. All letters will be used once.

I. $\dfrac{4}{5} = \dfrac{}{25}$

A. $\dfrac{3}{8} = \dfrac{}{64}$

G. $\dfrac{5}{6} = \dfrac{15}{}$

T. $\dfrac{7}{9} = \dfrac{}{36}$

Y. $\dfrac{3}{24} = \dfrac{}{8}$

H. $\dfrac{9}{18} = \dfrac{1}{}$

D. $\dfrac{30}{35} = \dfrac{6}{}$

L. $\dfrac{39}{52} = \dfrac{}{4}$

__ __ __ __ __ __ __ __

7   24   1   3   20   18   2   28

Saving Time began in the United States in 1918 to preserve daylight.

Write *yes* if each pair of fractions are equivalent. Write *no* if they are not equivalent. If they are not equivalent, write an equivalent fraction for the first fraction in the pair. If they are equivalent, write the number that you are multiplying or dividing by to make each equivalent fraction.

1. $\frac{2}{3}, \frac{8}{12}$

2. $\frac{4}{16}, \frac{1}{4}$

3. $\frac{5}{7}, \frac{25}{35}$

4. $\frac{7}{14}, \frac{3}{7}$

5. $\frac{10}{12}, \frac{20}{36}$

6. $\frac{3}{4}, \frac{36}{48}$

7. $\frac{12}{21}, \frac{4}{7}$

8. $\frac{18}{20}, \frac{9}{12}$

Find the missing numerator or denominator to write equivalent fractions.

9. $\frac{1}{2} = \frac{}{18}$

10. $\frac{24}{40} = \frac{}{5}$

11. $\frac{3}{7} = \frac{18}{}$

12. $\frac{14}{28} = \frac{7}{}$

13. $\dfrac{5}{9} = \dfrac{}{27}$

14. $\dfrac{3}{24} = \dfrac{1}{}$

15. $\dfrac{25}{50} = \dfrac{}{10}$

16. $\dfrac{7}{8} = \dfrac{56}{}$

Comparing fractions with like numerators or like denominators

The symbols > and < are inequality symbols. These inequality symbols and the equal sign can be used to compare fractions in the same way they are used to compare whole numbers, especially when the numerators or denominators of the fractions are the same.

The symbol > means "is greater than." The tip of this symbol points to the smaller number. For example, 5 > 2 is read "5 is greater than 2."

The symbol < means "is less than." The tip of this symbol points to the smaller number. For example 7 < 10 is read "7 is less than 10."

The = sign means "is equal to." The numbers on each side of this symbol have the same value.

Example 1: Use >, <, or = to compare $\dfrac{4}{5}$ and $\dfrac{2}{5}$.

- ◆ Because the denominators are the same, compare the numerators.
- ◆ The numerators are 4 and 2. Because 4 is greater than 2, $\dfrac{4}{5} > \dfrac{2}{5}$.

Example 2: Use >, <, or = to compare $\dfrac{1}{3}$ and $\dfrac{1}{5}$.

- ◆ Each numerator is 1, but the denominators are 3 and 5. For problems like this, find which denominator represents a larger part of the whole. The denominator that represents a larger part of the whole will represent the larger fraction when the numerators are equivalent. A model of this problem is shown in the figure that follows.

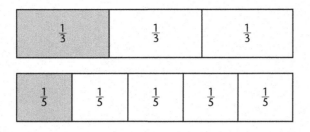

◆ Because $\frac{1}{3}$ represents a larger part of the whole, $\frac{1}{3} > \frac{1}{5}$.

EXERCISE 1·7

Circle the correct symbol to make each statement true. Write the letter under the symbol in the space above its problem number at the end of the exercise to complete the sentence. Some answers will be used more than once.

1. $\frac{3}{4}$ ———— $\frac{1}{4}$

    < > =

    P I D

2. $\frac{8}{11}$ ———— $\frac{8}{14}$

    < > =

    D K L

3. $\frac{5}{9}$ ———— $\frac{5}{12}$

    < > =

    E D N

4. $\frac{9}{17}$ ———— $\frac{9}{10}$

    < > =

    R S L

5. $\frac{1}{8}$ ———— $\frac{3}{8}$

    < > =

    C R K

6. $\dfrac{9}{12}$ —— $\dfrac{9}{12}$

    <   >   =

    J   T   Y

7. $\dfrac{6}{9}$ —— $\dfrac{6}{15}$

    <   >   =

    M   L   W

8. $\dfrac{13}{14}$ —— $\dfrac{7}{14}$

    <   >   =

    H   O   B

9. $\dfrac{4}{9}$ —— $\dfrac{4}{10}$

    <   >   =

    G   H   P

Andrew Jackson, the seventh president of the United States, gained his nickname

__   __   __   __   __   __   __   __   __   __

8   7   3   9   1   5   2   8   4   6

during the War of 1812.

EXERCISE
1·8

Use >, <, or = to compare each pair of fractions.

1. $\dfrac{6}{10}$ —— $\dfrac{6}{14}$

2. $\dfrac{11}{13}$ —— $\dfrac{6}{13}$

3. $\dfrac{7}{11}$ —— $\dfrac{5}{11}$

4. $\dfrac{15}{16}$ —— $\dfrac{15}{20}$

5. $\dfrac{8}{15}$ —— $\dfrac{9}{15}$

6. $\dfrac{2}{7}$ —— $\dfrac{2}{3}$

7. $\dfrac{4}{5}$ —— $\dfrac{4}{9}$

8. $\dfrac{1}{5}$ —— $\dfrac{2}{5}$

9. $\dfrac{11}{12}$ —— $\dfrac{12}{12}$

10. $\dfrac{16}{21}$ —— $\dfrac{16}{18}$

11. $\dfrac{8}{13}$ —— $\dfrac{8}{14}$

12. $\dfrac{9}{10}$ —— $\dfrac{4}{10}$

13. $\dfrac{1}{10}$ —— $\dfrac{1}{7}$

14. $\dfrac{7}{15}$ —— $\dfrac{8}{15}$

15. $\dfrac{9}{14}$ —— $\dfrac{9}{11}$

16. $\dfrac{17}{26}$ —— $\dfrac{16}{26}$

Comparing fractions with unlike numerators and unlike denominators

To compare fractions with unlike numerators and unlike denominators, you must find the least common multiple (LCM) of the denominators. This is called the least common denominator (LCD) of the fractions. You must then write equivalent fractions. Once you have found equivalent fractions with the same denominator, compare the fractions by determining which numerator is larger.

Example 1: Use >, <, or = to compare $\frac{5}{6}$ and $\frac{3}{4}$.

- ◆ Find the LCM of 6 and 4 by making a list or using prime factorization. The LCM of 6 and 4 is 12. 12 is the LCD of $\frac{5}{6}$ and $\frac{3}{4}$.

- ◆ Write equivalent fractions for $\frac{5}{6}$ and $\frac{3}{4}$ using the LCD, which is 12.

$$\frac{5}{6} = \frac{5 \times 2}{6 \times 2} = \frac{10}{12}$$

$$\frac{3}{4} = \frac{3 \times 3}{4 \times 3} = \frac{9}{12}$$

- ◆ Compare the numerators. Because 10 is greater than 9, $\frac{5}{6} > \frac{3}{4}$.

Example 2: Use >, <, or = to compare $\frac{2}{3}$ and $\frac{5}{8}$.

- ◆ Find the LCM of 3 and 8 by making a list or using prime factorization. The LCM of 3 and 8 is 24. 24 is the LCD of $\frac{2}{3}$ and $\frac{5}{8}$.

- ◆ Write equivalent fractions for $\frac{2}{3}$ and $\frac{5}{8}$ using the LCD, which is 24.

$$\frac{2}{3} = \frac{2 \times 8}{3 \times 8} = \frac{16}{24}$$

$$\frac{5}{8} = \frac{5 \times 3}{8 \times 3} = \frac{15}{24}$$

- ◆ Compare the numerators. Because 16 is greater than 15, $\frac{2}{3} > \frac{5}{8}$.

EXERCISE

1·9

Circle the symbol that makes each statement true. Write the letter under the symbol in the space above its problem number at the end of the exercise to complete the sentence. Some answers will be used more than once.

1. $\frac{2}{5}$ _____ $\frac{3}{10}$

    < > =

    G A T

2. $\dfrac{4}{5}$ —— $\dfrac{2}{3}$

    < > =

    H T O

3. $\dfrac{3}{4}$ —— $\dfrac{5}{6}$

    < > =

    L R A

4. $\dfrac{2}{4}$ —— $\dfrac{3}{7}$

    < > =

    U R W

5. $\dfrac{7}{12}$ —— $\dfrac{8}{9}$

    < > =

    I T M

6. $\dfrac{11}{12}$ —— $\dfrac{22}{24}$

    < > =

    K P U

7. $\dfrac{13}{15}$ —— $\dfrac{8}{12}$

    < > =

    I O U

8. $\dfrac{5}{8}$ —— $\dfrac{7}{12}$

    < > =

    M G T

9. $\dfrac{9}{10}$ —— $\dfrac{27}{30}$

    < > =

    D B C

10. $\dfrac{25}{48}$ ——— $\dfrac{4}{6}$

$<$ $>$ $=$

S   C   N

11. $\dfrac{7}{9}$ ——— $\dfrac{5}{8}$

$<$ $>$ $=$

J   N   R

The three main forms of fossil fuels are $\underline{}$ $\underline{}$ $\underline{}$ $\underline{}$, $\underline{}$ $\underline{}$ $\underline{}$,
$\quad$ 9 $\quad$ 7 $\quad$ 1 $\quad$ 3 $\quad$ 7 $\quad$ 5 $\quad$ 3

and $\underline{}$ $\underline{}$ $\underline{}$ $\underline{}$ $\underline{}$ $\underline{}$ $\underline{}$ $\quad$ $\underline{}$ $\underline{}$ $\underline{}$.
$\quad$ 11 $\quad$ 1 $\quad$ 2 $\quad$ 6 $\quad$ 4 $\quad$ 1 $\quad$ 3 $\qquad$ 8 $\quad$ 1 $\quad$ 10

They were formed before the time of the dinosaurs during the Carboniferous period.

◆
┌─────────┐
│ EXERCISE │
│ **1·10** │
└─────────┘

Use $>$, $<$, or $=$ to compare the fractions.

1. $\dfrac{5}{6}$ ——— $\dfrac{8}{12}$

2. $\dfrac{7}{10}$ ——— $\dfrac{14}{20}$

3. $\dfrac{7}{8}$ ——— $\dfrac{3}{4}$

4. $\dfrac{4}{9}$ ——— $\dfrac{3}{7}$

5. $\dfrac{4}{10}$ ——— $\dfrac{2}{4}$

6. $\dfrac{1}{3}$ ——— $\dfrac{2}{4}$

7. $\dfrac{7}{14}$ _____ $\dfrac{5}{7}$

8. $\dfrac{9}{27}$ _____ $\dfrac{1}{3}$

9. $\dfrac{5}{9}$ _____ $\dfrac{7}{12}$

10. $\dfrac{3}{4}$ _____ $\dfrac{5}{7}$

11. $\dfrac{11}{13}$ _____ $\dfrac{2}{3}$

12. $\dfrac{2}{6}$ _____ $\dfrac{4}{15}$

13. $\dfrac{12}{16}$ _____ $\dfrac{4}{6}$

14. $\dfrac{1}{5}$ _____ $\dfrac{2}{8}$

15. $\dfrac{4}{14}$ _____ $\dfrac{1}{3}$

16. $\dfrac{6}{16}$ _____ $\dfrac{5}{10}$

Ordering fractions

Ordering fractions is similar to comparing fractions. If the fractions have different denominators, you must find the least common denominator (LCD) and write equivalent fractions. You can then compare the numerators and place the fractions in order.

Example 1: Write the following fractions in order from least to greatest: $\dfrac{2}{3}$, $\dfrac{5}{6}$, $\dfrac{9}{12}$.

- ◆ First find the LCD of the fractions. The LCD is 12.

- ◆ Write equivalent fractions using the LCD. ($\dfrac{9}{12}$ already has a denominator of 12.)

$$\dfrac{2}{3} = \dfrac{2 \times 4}{3 \times 4} = \dfrac{8}{12}$$

$$\dfrac{5}{6} = \dfrac{5 \times 2}{6 \times 2} = \dfrac{10}{12}$$

◆ Because all of the denominators are now the same, compare the numerators. Place the numerators in order from least to greatest: 8, 9, and 10. Before writing the fractions in order from least to greatest, you must convert the equivalent fractions back to the original fractions in the problem. Because $\frac{2}{3} = \frac{8}{12}$, $\frac{9}{12} = \frac{9}{12}$, and $\frac{5}{6} = \frac{10}{12}$, the order of the fractions from least to greatest is $\frac{2}{3}$, $\frac{9}{12}$, $\frac{5}{6}$.

Example 2: Write the following fractions in order from greatest to least: $\frac{1}{4}$, $\frac{7}{10}$, $\frac{4}{5}$.

◆ Find the LCD of the fractions. The LCD is 20.

◆ Write equivalent fractions using the LCD.

$$\frac{1}{4} = \frac{1 \times 5}{4 \times 5} = \frac{5}{20}$$

$$\frac{7}{10} = \frac{7 \times 2}{10 \times 2} = \frac{14}{20}$$

$$\frac{4}{5} = \frac{4 \times 4}{5 \times 4} = \frac{16}{20}$$

◆ Now that all the denominators are equivalent, compare the numerators. Place the numerators in order from greatest to least: 16, 14, and 5. Because $\frac{4}{5} = \frac{16}{20}$, $\frac{7}{10} = \frac{14}{20}$, and $\frac{1}{4} = \frac{5}{20}$, the order of the fractions from greatest to least is $\frac{4}{5}$, $\frac{7}{10}$, $\frac{1}{4}$.

EXERCISE
1·11

Write each set of fractions (with their corresponding letters) in order from least to greatest. Write the letter of the middle number in each set in the space above its problem number at the end of the exercise to complete the sentence.

1. $\frac{3}{4}$, $\frac{1}{2}$, $\frac{5}{8}$

  K E L

2. $\frac{5}{8}$, $\frac{7}{12}$, $\frac{5}{6}$

  R H B

3. $\frac{7}{8}$, $\frac{2}{3}$, $\frac{1}{2}$

  C O N

4. $\frac{1}{3}$, $\frac{2}{9}$, $\frac{1}{18}$

  E D S

5. $\dfrac{4}{5}, \dfrac{7}{10}, \dfrac{6}{15}$

    R   C   T

6. $\dfrac{4}{6}, \dfrac{3}{4}, \dfrac{1}{2}$

    Y W G

<u>   </u> <u>   </u> <u>   </u>   <u>   </u> <u>   </u> <u>   </u> <u>   </u> <u>   </u> is created by the amount and type of

 4   6   4   5   3   1   3   2

pigment in the iris.

EXERCISE 1·12

Write each set of fractions in order from least to greatest.

1. $\dfrac{5}{6}, \dfrac{1}{4}, \dfrac{3}{5}$

2. $\dfrac{2}{5}, \dfrac{4}{6}, \dfrac{2}{4}$

3. $\dfrac{4}{10}, \dfrac{1}{3}, \dfrac{4}{5}$

4. $\dfrac{1}{3}, \dfrac{2}{9}, \dfrac{1}{18}$

5. $\dfrac{5}{12}, \dfrac{1}{6}, \dfrac{3}{8}$

6. $\dfrac{4}{6}, \dfrac{3}{7}, \dfrac{10}{14}$

7. $\dfrac{3}{4}, \dfrac{5}{9}, \dfrac{7}{12}$

8. $\dfrac{13}{20}, \dfrac{7}{8}, \dfrac{3}{5}$

Write each set of fractions in order from greatest to least.

9. $\dfrac{10}{12}, \dfrac{5}{9}, \dfrac{3}{4}$

10. $\dfrac{3}{10}, \dfrac{2}{6}, \dfrac{5}{12}$

11. $\dfrac{4}{8}, \dfrac{12}{16}, \dfrac{45}{64}$

12. $\dfrac{14}{21}, \dfrac{12}{13}, \dfrac{4}{5}$

13. $\dfrac{2}{6}, \dfrac{3}{10}, \dfrac{2}{7}$

14. $\dfrac{4}{9}, \dfrac{7}{18}, \dfrac{5}{6}$

15. $\dfrac{11}{14}, \dfrac{3}{7}, \dfrac{6}{8}$

16. $\dfrac{27}{30}, \dfrac{11}{12}, \dfrac{3}{4}$

Finding the greatest common factor (GCF)

A factor is a number that divides into another number evenly. For example, the factors of 10 are 1, 2, 5, and 10 because $1 \times 10 = 10$ and $2 \times 5 = 10$ (or, because division and multiplication are inverse operations, $10 \div 1 = 10$ and $10 \div 2 = 5$).

A common factor of two numbers is a factor that is shared by the numbers. The greatest common factor (GCF) of two numbers is the largest factor that is common to both numbers.

There are two methods for finding the GCF: making a list and using prime factorization.

Method 1: Make a list

Example 1: Find the GCF of 24 and 60.

◆ Make a list of the factors of 24 and 60.

The factors of 24: 1, 2, 3, 4, 6, 8, 12, 24

The factors of 60: 1, 2, 3, 4, 5, 6, 10, 12, 15, 20, 30, 60

◆ When listing factors, it is helpful to begin with 1 and write pairs of factors. For example, 1 × 24 = 24. Then write the next consecutive factor. For example, 2 × 12 = 24. Continue this process until you have listed all the possible factors of 24.

◆ Once your list is complete, find the common factors. In this example, common factors of 24 and 60 are 1, 2, 3, 4, 6, and 12. The largest of these common factors is 12. 12 is the GCF of 24 and 60.

Example 2: Find the GCF of 36 and 45.

◆ Make a list of the factors of 36 and 45.

The factors of 36: 1, 2, 3, 4, 6, 9, 12, 18, 36

The factors of 45: 1, 3, 5, 9, 15, 45

◆ The common factors of 36 and 45 are 1, 3, and 9. The GCF of 36 and 45 is 9.

Method 2: Use prime factorization

Prime factorization is the process of writing a number as the product of its prime factors. Prime numbers have only two factors, 1 and the number. Composite numbers have more than two factors.

To use prime factorization to find the GCF, create a factor tree. Write one of the numbers at the top of the tree. Factor this number. Then factor the factors until the last number on each branch of prime number. Follow the same procedure with the second number. Once you have found the prime factorization of both numbers, find the product of the common factors to find the GCF.

Example: Find the GCF of 48 and 52.

◆ Make a factor tree for each number. For 48, start with 2 and 24. (You can also start with other factors of 48.) For 52, start with 2 and 26. (You can also start with other factors of 52.)

◆ Because 24 and 26 are composite numbers, they must be factored. Factor 24 as 2 × 12 and factor 26 as 2 × 13.

◆ Because the factors of 52 are 2, 2, and 13 are all prime numbers, this factor tree is complete. The prime factorization of 52 is 2 × 2 × 13. The prime factorization of 48 is incomplete because 12 is a composite number. Factor 12 as 2 × 6.

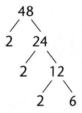

◆ Because 6 is a composite number, factor 6 as 2 × 3.

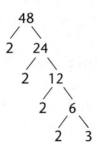

◆ The end of every branch of the factor tree for 48 now has a prime number. The prime factorization of 48 is complete and is equal to 2 × 2 × 2 × 2 × 3. As noted previously, the prime factorization of 52 is 2 × 2 × 13.

◆ Find the common factors. Both sets of prime factorizations have two 2s. Find the product of the common factors by multiplying 2 × 2 to get 4, which is the GCF of 48 and 52.

Find the GCF of each pair of numbers using the given method. Write the letter of the problem in the space above its answer at the end of the exercise to complete the sentence. Some answers will be used twice. Some answers will not be used.

Make a list to find the GCF of each pair of numbers.

R. 36 and 42

S. 62 and 31

M. 56 and 70

C. 90 and 40

D. 25 and 30

U. 84 and 96

Use prime factorization to find the GCF of each pair of numbers.

H. 75 and 100

T. 45 and 33

E. 121 and 88

L. 148 and 74

O. 59 and 83

N. 120 and 90

—	—	—	—	—	—	—	—	—	—	—	are found in the
10	25	6	1	14	1	31	1	14	11	31	

—	—	—	—	—	—	—	of a cell.
30	12	10	74	11	12	31	

EXERCISE 1·14

Make a list to find the GCF of each pair of numbers.

1. 38 and 40

2. 18 and 9

3. 55 and 70

4. 39 and 13

5. 24 and 36

6. 56 and 66

7. 81 and 54

8. 91 and 33

Use prime factorization to find the GCF of each pair of numbers.

9. 14 and 20

10. 28 and 36

11. 49 and 21

12. 44 and 82

13. 88 and 100

14. 18 and 76

15. 135 and 49

16. 115 and 75

Simplest form

A fraction is in simplest form when the numerator and denominator have no common factors greater than 1. Follow the steps below to simplify fractions.

1. Find the GCF of the numerator and denominator by making a list or using prime factorization.

2. Divide the numerator and denominator by the GCF.

3. Check that your fraction is in simplest form by finding that 1 is the only common factor of the numerator and denominator.

Example 1: Write $\frac{6}{10}$ in simplest form.

- Find the GCF of 6 and 10. The GCF is 2.
- Divide the numerator and denominator by 2. $\frac{6}{10} = \frac{6 \div 2}{10 \div 2} = \frac{3}{5}$
- $\frac{3}{5}$ is in simplest form because 3 and 5 have no common factors other than 1.

Example 2: Write $\frac{15}{20}$ in simplest form.

- Find the GCF of 15 and 20. The GCF is 5.
- Divide the numerator and denominator by 5. $\frac{15}{20} = \frac{15 \div 5}{20 \div 5} = \frac{3}{4}$
- $\frac{3}{4}$ is in simplest form because 3 and 4 have no common factors other than 1.

Simplify each fraction. Write the letter of the fraction in the space above its simplest form at the end of the exercise to complete the sentence. Some letters will be used more than once. Some letters will not be used.

H. $\dfrac{5}{10}$

E. $\dfrac{8}{10}$

F. $\dfrac{7}{21}$

I. $\dfrac{35}{45}$

J. $\dfrac{20}{30}$

P. $\dfrac{21}{33}$

O. $\dfrac{18}{30}$

S. $\dfrac{44}{50}$

N. $\dfrac{28}{30}$

C. $\dfrac{30}{36}$

___ ___ ___ ___ ___ ___ ___ ___ ___ ___ ___, a widely respected Native
$\frac{5}{6}$ $\frac{1}{2}$ $\frac{7}{9}$ $\frac{4}{5}$ $\frac{1}{3}$ $\frac{2}{3}$ $\frac{3}{5}$ $\frac{22}{25}$ $\frac{4}{5}$ $\frac{7}{11}$ $\frac{1}{2}$

American, was the last leader of the Nez Percé. The Nez Percé occupied much of the Plains and Rocky Mountains during the 1800s.

Write each fraction in simplest form.

1. $\dfrac{9}{21}$

2. $\dfrac{9}{21}$

3. $\dfrac{10}{30}$

4. $\dfrac{12}{18}$

5. $\dfrac{15}{60}$

6. $\dfrac{40}{55}$

7. $\dfrac{4}{20}$

8. $\dfrac{15}{24}$

9. $\dfrac{10}{16}$

10. $\dfrac{25}{30}$

11. $\dfrac{28}{32}$

12. $\dfrac{4}{24}$

13. $\dfrac{36}{42}$

14. $\dfrac{8}{18}$

15. $\dfrac{14}{38}$

16. $\dfrac{81}{90}$

Converting improper fractions to mixed numbers and mixed numbers to improper fractions

An improper fraction is a fraction in which the numerator is greater than the denominator. An improper fraction is greater than 1. For example, $\frac{7}{4}$ is an improper fraction. A model of $\frac{7}{4}$ is shown in the following figure.

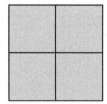 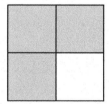

An improper fraction can be expressed as a mixed number or as a whole number. A mixed number consists of a whole number and a fraction. In the model of $\frac{7}{4}$, the first large square is divided into 4 equal parts. The 4 shaded parts equal 1 whole. This 1 whole can also be thought of as $\frac{4}{4}$ because 4 out of the 4 parts are shaded. In the second large square, only 3 out of the 4 parts are shaded, representing $\frac{3}{4}$. The total shaded parts, $\frac{7}{4}$, can also be written as $1\frac{3}{4}$, which is a mixed number. In $1\frac{3}{4}$, the 1 represents the one whole square that is shaded. The $\frac{3}{4}$ represents the three out of four squares shaded in the second square. $\frac{7}{4}$ and $1\frac{3}{4}$ are equivalent because they represent the same amount.

Follow these steps for converting an improper fraction to a mixed number:

1. Divide the numerator by the denominator.

2. Write the quotient as the whole number.

3. Write the remainder as the numerator of a fraction over the original denominator.

4. Simplify the fraction, if necessary. If there is no remainder, the improper fraction is a whole number.

Example 1: Change $\frac{9}{2}$ to a mixed number.

- Divide the numerator by the denominator.

$$2\overline{)9}^{\textstyle 4}$$
$$\underline{8}$$
$$1$$

- The quotient, 4, is the whole number. The remainder, 1, is the numerator of the fraction. The denominator stays the same.

- $\frac{9}{2} = 4\frac{1}{2}$ The fraction is in simplest form.

Example 2: Change $\frac{20}{6}$ to a mixed number.

- Divide the numerator by the denominator.

$$6\overline{)20}^{\textstyle 3}$$
$$\underline{18}$$
$$2$$

- The quotient, 3, is the whole number. The remainder, 2, is the numerator of the fraction. The denominator is 6. But the fraction, $\frac{2}{6}$, is not in simplest form. Divide the numerator and the denominator by the GCF, which is 2. $\frac{2}{6} = \frac{1}{3}$

- $\frac{20}{6} = 3\frac{2}{6} = 3\frac{1}{3}$ The fraction is in simplest form.

You can change mixed numbers into improper fractions by following these directions:

1. Multiply the whole number by the denominator.

2. Add the numerator to the product.

3. Write the sum as the new numerator. Use the original denominator.

Example 1: Change $3\frac{1}{5}$ to an improper fraction.

- Multiply the whole number by the denominator. $3 \times 5 = 15$

- Add the numerator to the product. $1 + 15 = 16$

- 16 is the new numerator. 5 is the denominator. $3\frac{1}{5} = \frac{16}{5}$

Example 2: Change $4\frac{7}{8}$ to an improper fraction.

- Multiply the whole number by the denominator. $4 \times 8 = 32$

- Add the numerator to the product. $32 + 7 = 39$

- 39 is the new numerator. 8 is the denominator. $4\frac{7}{8} = \frac{39}{8}$

Change each improper fraction to a mixed number and change each mixed number to an improper fraction. Write the letter of each fraction in the space above its answer at the end of the exercise to complete the sentence. Some letters will be used more than once. Some letters will not be used.

A. $\dfrac{24}{5}$

N. $\dfrac{17}{3}$

I. $\dfrac{30}{4}$

T. $\dfrac{17}{4}$

C. $\dfrac{21}{3}$

O. $\dfrac{53}{6}$

R. $4\dfrac{3}{4}$

S. $6\dfrac{1}{3}$

M. $6\dfrac{1}{2}$

L. $7\dfrac{1}{7}$

E. $8\dfrac{5}{8}$

P. $5\dfrac{1}{3}$

In 1863, President Abraham Lincoln issued the

$$\frac{69}{8} \quad \frac{13}{2} \quad 4\frac{4}{5} \quad 5\frac{2}{3} \quad 7 \quad 7\frac{1}{2} \quad \frac{16}{3} \quad 4\frac{4}{5} \quad 4\frac{1}{4} \quad 7\frac{1}{2} \quad 8\frac{5}{6} \quad 5\frac{2}{3}$$

$$\frac{16}{3} \quad \frac{19}{4} \quad 8\frac{5}{6} \quad 7 \quad \frac{50}{7} \quad 4\frac{4}{5} \quad \frac{13}{2} \quad 4\frac{4}{5} \quad 4\frac{1}{4} \quad 7\frac{1}{2} \quad 8\frac{5}{6} \quad 5\frac{2}{3},$$

which freed all slaves in all states still at war with the Union.

EXERCISE
1·18

Convert each improper fraction to a mixed number or a whole number.

1. $\dfrac{15}{4}$

2. $\dfrac{8}{3}$

3. $\dfrac{27}{5}$

4. $\dfrac{51}{10}$

5. $\dfrac{36}{6}$

6. $\dfrac{33}{9}$

7. $\dfrac{49}{8}$

8. $\dfrac{80}{8}$

Convert each mixed number to an improper fraction.

9. $3\frac{4}{5}$

10. $1\frac{5}{6}$

11. $4\frac{1}{3}$

12. $7\frac{9}{10}$

13. $5\frac{5}{9}$

14. $4\frac{3}{8}$

15. $6\frac{10}{11}$

16. $8\frac{1}{9}$

Operations with fractions

Estimating sums and differences of fractions

Because operations with fractions can be challenging, it is helpful to estimate your solution before finding your answer. An estimate is an answer that is close to the exact answer. It is found by rounding. By estimating first, you will be able to tell if your answer is reasonable.

When estimating the sums or differences of fractions, it is helpful to use benchmarks. Benchmarks are numbers that fractions can be rounded to, such as 0, $\frac{1}{2}$, and 1.

Examples of fractions that can be rounded to 0 include $\frac{1}{10}$, $\frac{1}{9}$, $\frac{1}{5}$, $\frac{3}{13}$. In each of these fractions, the numerator is much less than the denominator.

Examples of fractions that can be rounded to $\frac{1}{2}$ include $\frac{5}{11}$, $\frac{3}{8}$, $\frac{4}{9}$, $\frac{3}{7}$. In each of these fractions, the numerator is about half of the denominator.

Examples of fractions that can be rounded to 1 include $\frac{4}{5}$, $\frac{9}{10}$, $\frac{14}{17}$, $\frac{8}{9}$. In each of these fractions, the numerator is about the same as the denominator.

To estimate sums or differences of fractions, first round each fraction to 0, $\frac{1}{2}$, or 1. Then add or subtract your estimates. This will give you an estimate of your actual answer.

Example 1: Estimate the sum of $\frac{8}{9} + \frac{1}{4}$.

- ◆ Round each fraction to 0, $\frac{1}{2}$ or 1. $\frac{8}{9}$ is close to 1 and $\frac{1}{4}$ is close to 0.
- ◆ Rewrite the problem as $1 + 0$.
- ◆ Add. $1 + 0 = 1$
- ◆ $\frac{8}{9} + \frac{1}{4}$ is about 1.

Example 2: Estimate the difference of $\frac{5}{6} - \frac{4}{9}$.

- ◆ Round each fraction to 0, $\frac{1}{2}$, or 1. $\frac{5}{6}$ is close to 1 and $\frac{4}{9}$ is close to $\frac{1}{2}$.
- ◆ Rewrite the problem as $1 - \frac{1}{2}$.
- ◆ Subtract. $1 - \frac{1}{2} = \frac{1}{2}$
- ◆ $\frac{5}{6} - \frac{4}{9}$ is about $\frac{1}{2}$.

Round each fraction to 0, $\frac{1}{2}$, or 1.

1. $\frac{11}{12}$

2. $\frac{3}{7}$

3. $\frac{1}{5}$

4. $\frac{5}{8}$

5. $\frac{2}{9}$

6. $\frac{6}{10}$

Estimate each sum or difference.

7. $\frac{4}{5} + \frac{2}{6}$

8. $\frac{5}{8} - \frac{5}{12}$

9. $\frac{1}{15} + \frac{4}{9}$

10. $\frac{7}{8} - \frac{4}{9}$

11. $\frac{11}{13} - \frac{9}{10}$

12. $\frac{1}{9} + \frac{13}{15}$

13. $\frac{3}{8} - \frac{6}{10}$

14. $\frac{13}{14} + \frac{10}{18}$

15. $\frac{19}{21} + \frac{12}{17}$

16. $\frac{14}{17} - \frac{2}{9}$

Addition and subtraction of fractions (like denominators)

When two fractions have the same denominator, they are said to have "like denominators." To add or subtract fractions with like denominators, add or subtract the numerators, but leave the denominator the same. Remember to write the fraction in simplest form and convert any improper fractions to mixed numbers.

Example 1: $\frac{4}{7} + \frac{2}{7}$

- Because $\frac{4}{7}$ and $\frac{2}{7}$ both have the denominator of 7, they are said to have like denominators.

- Add the numerators, 4 + 2, for a sum of 6.

- Leave the denominator as 7.

- The answer is $\frac{6}{7}$, which is in simplest form.

The following figure represents example 1. The whole is divided into 7 equal parts. Each part represents $\frac{1}{7}$ of the whole. The first 4 parts are shaded in light gray, which represent a total of $\frac{4}{7}$. Two of the parts are shaded in dark gray, which represent $\frac{2}{7}$. All together, 6 out of 7 boxes are shaded, representing $\frac{6}{7}$. The arrow shows that you have added $\frac{2}{7}$ to $\frac{4}{7}$ for a total of $\frac{6}{7}$.

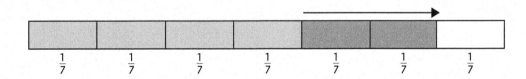

Example 2: $\frac{9}{10} - \frac{4}{10}$

- Because 10 is the denominator in both fractions, subtract the numerators. 9 − 4 = 5

- Leave the denominator as 10.

- ◆ The answer is $\frac{5}{10}$, which can be simplified by dividing the numerator and denominator by 5. $\frac{5}{10} = \frac{5 \div 5}{10 \div 5} = \frac{1}{2}$
- ◆ The answer is $\frac{1}{2}$.

The following figure represents example 2. The whole is divided into 10 equal parts. Each part represents $\frac{1}{10}$ of the whole. 9 out of 10 parts are shaded, which represent the first fraction, $\frac{9}{10}$. Because you are subtracting, or taking away, $\frac{4}{10}$, an arrow pointing left is drawn above 4 of the 9 shaded boxes. When you take away these $\frac{4}{10}$, you are left with $\frac{5}{10}$, which can be simplified to $\frac{1}{2}$.

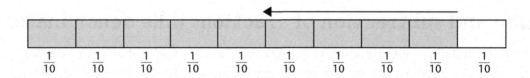

Add or subtract. Simplify, if necessary.

1. $\frac{1}{4} + \frac{1}{4}$

2. $\frac{2}{5} + \frac{1}{5}$

3. $\frac{5}{8} - \frac{1}{8}$

4. $\frac{8}{9} - \frac{5}{9}$

5. $\frac{6}{7} - \frac{2}{7}$

6. $\frac{7}{11} + \frac{3}{11}$

7. $\frac{3}{10} + \frac{1}{10}$

8. $\frac{1}{15} + \frac{4}{9}$

9. $\dfrac{11}{12} - \dfrac{7}{12}$

10. $\dfrac{5}{9} - \dfrac{1}{9}$

11. $\dfrac{8}{13} - \dfrac{4}{13}$

12. $\dfrac{4}{5} + \dfrac{2}{5}$

13. $\dfrac{9}{17} - \dfrac{8}{17}$

14. $\dfrac{12}{13} - \dfrac{4}{13}$

15. $\dfrac{13}{18} + \dfrac{3}{18}$

16. $\dfrac{8}{9} + \dfrac{4}{9}$

Addition of fractions (unlike denominators)

To add fractions with unlike denominators, you must first find a common denominator. Follow these steps:

1. Find the least common denominator (LCD) of the fractions. (Remember, this is the same as finding the least common multiple, or LCM, of the denominators.)

2. Write equivalent fractions, using the LCD. Multiply the numerator and denominator by the same number so that the denominator of each fraction is equivalent to the LCD.

3. Add the fractions as you would add fractions with like denominators. Add the numerators and leave the denominators the same.

4. Write the answer in its simplest form.

Example 1: $\dfrac{3}{4} + \dfrac{1}{6}$

- Find the LCD of the fractions. The LCD is 12.

- Write equivalent fractions using the LCD. $\dfrac{3}{4} = \dfrac{3 \times 3}{4 \times 3} = \dfrac{9}{12}$ and $\dfrac{1}{6} = \dfrac{1 \times 2}{6 \times 2} = \dfrac{2}{12}$

◆ Add. $\frac{9}{12} + \frac{2}{12}$

◆ The answer is $\frac{11}{12}$, which is in simplest form.

Example 2: $\frac{4}{5} + \frac{2}{3}$

◆ Find the LCD of the fractions. The LCD is 15.

◆ Write an equivalent fraction using the LCD. $\frac{4}{5} = \frac{4 \times 3}{5 \times 3} = \frac{12}{15}$ and $\frac{2}{3} = \frac{2 \times 5}{3 \times 5} = \frac{10}{15}$

◆ Add. $\frac{12}{15} + \frac{10}{15} = \frac{22}{15}$

◆ $\frac{22}{15}$ can be simplified to $1\frac{7}{15}$.

EXERCISE 2·3

Add. Simplify, if necessary. Write the letter of the problem in the space above its answer at the end of the exercise to complete the sentence. Some answers will be used twice. Some answers will not be used.

E. $\quad \frac{2}{9} + \frac{2}{3}$

I. $\quad \frac{1}{8} + \frac{3}{10}$

P. $\quad \frac{5}{6} + \frac{1}{4}$

N. $\quad \frac{3}{5} + \frac{5}{6}$

A. $\quad \frac{10}{11} + \frac{1}{3}$

M. $\quad \frac{7}{12} + \frac{7}{8}$

J. $\quad \frac{4}{5} + \frac{2}{9}$

S. $\quad \frac{1}{7} + \frac{2}{8}$

The word *sayonara* means "good-bye" in $\underline{}\ \underline{}\ \underline{}\ \underline{}\ \underline{}\ \underline{}\ \underline{}\ \underline{}$.

$\quad 1\frac{1}{45} \quad 1\frac{8}{33} \quad 1\frac{1}{12} \quad 1\frac{8}{33} \quad 1\frac{13}{30} \quad \frac{8}{9} \quad \frac{11}{28} \quad \frac{8}{9}$

Add. Simplify, if necessary.

1. $\dfrac{2}{4} + \dfrac{1}{8}$

2. $\dfrac{3}{5} + \dfrac{3}{10}$

3. $\dfrac{7}{9} + \dfrac{1}{2}$

4. $\dfrac{5}{6} + \dfrac{1}{9}$

5. $\dfrac{3}{7} + \dfrac{1}{6}$

6. $\dfrac{4}{11} + \dfrac{1}{2}$

7. $\dfrac{6}{11} + \dfrac{3}{4}$

8. $\dfrac{7}{10} + \dfrac{5}{8}$

9. $\dfrac{5}{12} + \dfrac{3}{8}$

10. $\dfrac{5}{14} + \dfrac{5}{6}$

11. $\dfrac{2}{9} + \dfrac{22}{27}$

12. $\dfrac{8}{15} + \dfrac{2}{9}$

13. $\dfrac{2}{15} + \dfrac{3}{20}$

14. $\dfrac{1}{16} + \dfrac{1}{4}$

15. $\frac{7}{13} + \frac{2}{3}$

16. $\frac{19}{21} + \frac{2}{3}$

Subtraction of fractions (unlike denominators)

Subtracting fractions with unlike denominators is similar to adding fractions with unlike denominators. Follow the steps presented here to subtract fractions with unlike denominators.

1. Find the least common denominator (LCD) of the fractions.

2. Write equivalent fractions, using the LCD. Multiply the numerator and denominator by the same number so that the denominator of each fraction is equivalent to the LCD.

3. Subtract the fractions as you would subtract fractions with like denominators. Subtract the numerators and leave the denominators the same.

4. Write the answer in simplest form.

Example 1: $\frac{3}{4} - \frac{3}{8}$

◆ Find the LCD of the fractions. The LCD is 8.

◆ Rewrite $\frac{3}{4}$ as $\frac{6}{8}$. $\frac{3}{4} = \frac{3 \times 2}{4 \times 2} = \frac{6}{8}$. Because $\frac{3}{8}$ already has the LCD as its denominator, it remains $\frac{3}{8}$.

◆ Rewrite the problem as $\frac{6}{8} - \frac{3}{8}$ and subtract.

◆ The answer is $\frac{3}{8}$, which is in simplest form.

Example 2: $\frac{4}{5} - \frac{1}{6}$

◆ Find the LCD of the fractions. The LCD is 30.

◆ Rewrite $\frac{4}{5}$ as $\frac{24}{30}$. $\frac{4}{5} = \frac{4 \times 6}{5 \times 6} = \frac{24}{30}$. Rewrite $\frac{1}{6}$ as $\frac{5}{30}$. $\frac{1}{6} = \frac{1 \times 5}{6 \times 5} = \frac{5}{30}$

◆ Rewrite the problem as $\frac{24}{30} \times \frac{5}{30}$ and subtract.

◆ The answer is $\frac{19}{30}$, which is in simplest form.

Subtract. Simplify, if necessary. Write the letter of the problem in the space above its answer at the end of the exercise to complete the sentence. Some answers will be used twice. Some answers will not be used.

O. $\dfrac{5}{8} - \dfrac{1}{4}$

S. $\dfrac{7}{10} - \dfrac{1}{2}$

N. $\dfrac{5}{7} - \dfrac{1}{6}$

T. $\dfrac{7}{8} - \dfrac{2}{5}$

U. $\dfrac{11}{12} - \dfrac{4}{15}$

L. $\dfrac{2}{5} - \dfrac{1}{7}$

I. $\dfrac{6}{9} - \dfrac{3}{6}$

C. $\dfrac{12}{20} - \dfrac{3}{9}$

Although many of us celebrate the year 1776, the

$\overline{\rule{1.2em}{0pt}}$ $\overline{\rule{1.2em}{0pt}}$ $\overline{\rule{1.2em}{0pt}}$ $\overline{\rule{1.2em}{0pt}}$ $\overline{\rule{1.2em}{0pt}}$ $\overline{\rule{1.2em}{0pt}}$ $\overline{\rule{1.2em}{0pt}}$ $\overline{\rule{1.2em}{0pt}}$ $\overline{\rule{1.2em}{0pt}}$ $\overline{\rule{1.2em}{0pt}}$ $\overline{\rule{1.2em}{0pt}}$ $\overline{\rule{1.2em}{0pt}}$

$\dfrac{4}{15}$ $\quad$ $\dfrac{3}{8}$ $\quad$ $\dfrac{23}{42}$ $\quad$ $\dfrac{1}{5}$ $\quad$ $\dfrac{19}{40}$ $\quad$ $\dfrac{1}{6}$ $\quad$ $\dfrac{19}{40}$ $\quad$ $\dfrac{13}{20}$ $\quad$ $\dfrac{19}{40}$ $\quad$ $\dfrac{1}{6}$ $\quad$ $\dfrac{3}{8}$ $\quad$ $\dfrac{23}{42}$

of the United States did not go into effect until 1789.

Subtract. Simplify, if necessary.

1. $\dfrac{6}{7} - \dfrac{1}{2}$

2. $\dfrac{8}{9} - \dfrac{2}{4}$

3. $\dfrac{9}{10} - \dfrac{2}{5}$

4. $\dfrac{5}{6} - \dfrac{1}{12}$

5. $\dfrac{2}{3} - \dfrac{2}{9}$

6. $\dfrac{6}{8} - \dfrac{2}{3}$

7. $\dfrac{3}{4} - \dfrac{1}{3}$

8. $\dfrac{5}{9} - \dfrac{1}{2}$

9. $\dfrac{7}{10} - \dfrac{2}{5}$

10. $\dfrac{7}{12} - \dfrac{1}{3}$

11. $\dfrac{13}{15} - \dfrac{4}{9}$

12. $\dfrac{13}{14} - \dfrac{3}{28}$

13. $\dfrac{5}{7} - \dfrac{1}{4}$

14. $\dfrac{7}{8} - \dfrac{3}{5}$

15. $\dfrac{11}{12} - \dfrac{3}{8}$

16. $\dfrac{8}{11} - \dfrac{2}{6}$

Addition and subtraction of fractions and mixed numbers (like denominators)

The process for adding and subtracting fractions and mixed numbers with like denominators is similar to adding and subtracting fractions with like denominators. Follow these steps:

1. Rewrite the problem vertically, if necessary. This creates one column for the fractions and another for whole numbers.

2. Add or subtract the like fractions. Remember that when adding or subtracting fractions with like denominators, only add or subtract the numerators. The denominators remain the same.

3. Add or subtract the whole numbers.

4. Write the fraction or mixed number in simplest form.

Example 1: $3\dfrac{3}{4} + 2\dfrac{3}{4}$

- Rewrite the problem vertically.

$$\begin{array}{r} 3\frac{3}{4} \\ + \ 2\frac{3}{4} \\ \hline \end{array}$$

- Add the fractions.

$$\begin{array}{r} 3\frac{3}{4} \\ + \ 2\frac{3}{4} \\ \hline \frac{6}{4} \end{array}$$

- Add the whole numbers.

$$\begin{array}{r} 3\frac{3}{4} \\ + \ 2\frac{3}{4} \\ \hline 5\frac{6}{4} \end{array}$$

◆ Write the mixed number in simplest form. First simplify the fraction.
$\frac{6}{4} = 1\frac{2}{4} = 1\frac{1}{2}$ Add the whole numbers. $5 + 1\frac{1}{2} = 6\frac{1}{2}$

◆ $6\frac{1}{2}$ is the answer in simplest form.

Example 2: $3\frac{3}{5} - 1\frac{1}{5}$

◆ Rewrite the problem vertically.

$$3\frac{3}{5}$$
$$- 1\frac{1}{5}$$
$$\overline{}$$

◆ Subtract $\frac{1}{5}$ from $\frac{3}{5}$ to find $\frac{2}{5}$.

$$3\frac{3}{5}$$
$$- 1\frac{1}{5}$$
$$\overline{}$$
$$\frac{2}{5}$$

◆ Subtract the whole numbers, 1 from 3 to find 2.

$$3\frac{3}{5}$$
$$- 1\frac{1}{5}$$
$$\overline{}$$
$$2\frac{2}{5}$$

◆ $2\frac{2}{5}$ is the answer in simplest form.

EXERCISE
2·7

Add or subtract. Simplify, if necessary.

1. $2\frac{1}{2} + 1\frac{1}{2}$

2. $4\frac{2}{7} - 3\frac{1}{7}$

3. $4\frac{4}{5} - 2\frac{2}{5}$

4. $8\frac{2}{3} + \frac{2}{3}$

5. $2\frac{5}{9} - \frac{2}{9}$

6. $7\frac{3}{10} - 5\frac{1}{10}$

7. $5\frac{1}{6} + \frac{5}{6}$

8. $5\frac{7}{8} + 2\frac{3}{8}$

9. $4\frac{11}{12} - 3\frac{8}{12}$

10. $\frac{4}{9} + 2\frac{4}{9}$

11. $1\frac{8}{9} - \frac{7}{9}$

12. $10\frac{3}{4} - 7\frac{1}{4}$

13. $7\frac{3}{5} + 3\frac{1}{5}$

14. $8\frac{6}{7} - \frac{2}{7}$

15. $2\frac{6}{9} + 1\frac{3}{9}$

16. $3\frac{10}{13} + 4\frac{12}{13}$

Addition of fractions and mixed numbers (unlike denominators)

To add fractions and mixed numbers with unlike denominators, you must first find common denominators. Follow these steps:

1. Rewrite the problem vertically, if necessary.

2. Find the least common denominator (LCD) of the fractions.

3. Write equivalent fractions. Leave the whole numbers as they are.

4. Add the fractions.

5. Add the whole numbers.

6. Write the sum in simplest form.

Example 1: $3\frac{3}{4} + 1\frac{1}{2}$

- Rewrite the problem vertically.

$$3\frac{3}{4}$$
$$+ 1\frac{1}{2}$$
$$\overline{}$$

- Find the LCD of the fractions. The LCD is 4. $3\frac{3}{4}$ stays the same because the denominator is already 4. Using the LCD, write an equivalent fraction for $1\frac{1}{2}$. $1\frac{1}{2}$ is equivalent to $1\frac{2}{4}$. (Remember that the whole number remains the same.) $\frac{1}{2} = \frac{1\times2}{2\times2} = \frac{2}{4}$

- Rewrite the problem using the equivalent fractions.

$$3\frac{3}{4}$$
$$+ 1\frac{2}{4}$$
$$\overline{}$$

- Add the fractions.

$$3\frac{3}{4}$$
$$+ 1\frac{2}{4}$$
$$\overline{}$$
$$\frac{5}{4}$$

- Add the whole numbers.

$$3\frac{3}{4}$$
$$+ 1\frac{2}{4}$$
$$\overline{}$$
$$4\frac{5}{4}$$

- Simplify the fraction. $\frac{5}{4} = 1\frac{1}{4}$
- Add the whole numbers. $4 + 1\frac{1}{4} = 5\frac{1}{4}$
- $5\frac{1}{4}$ is the answer in simplest form.

Example 2: $3\frac{1}{5} + 4\frac{1}{3}$

- ◆ Rewrite the problem vertically.

$$3\tfrac{1}{5}$$
$$+\ 4\tfrac{1}{3}$$

- ◆ Find the LCD of the fractions. The LCD is 15. $3\tfrac{1}{5}$ is equivalent to $3\tfrac{3}{15}$ and $4\tfrac{1}{3}$ is equivalent to $4\tfrac{5}{15}$.

- ◆ Rewrite the problem using the equivalent fractions.

$$3\tfrac{3}{15}$$
$$+\ 4\tfrac{5}{15}$$

- ◆ Add the fractions.

$$3\tfrac{3}{15}$$
$$+\ 4\tfrac{5}{15}$$
$$\tfrac{8}{15}$$

- ◆ Add the whole numbers.

$$3\tfrac{3}{15}$$
$$+\ 4\tfrac{5}{15}$$
$$7\tfrac{8}{15}$$

- ◆ $7\tfrac{8}{15}$ is the sum, which is in simplest form.

EXERCISE 2·8

Add. Simplify, if necessary. Write the letter of the problem in the space above its answer at the end of the exercise to complete the sentence. Some answers will be used more than once.

A. $2\tfrac{1}{5} + 2\tfrac{3}{10}$

E. $1\tfrac{4}{7} + 2\tfrac{1}{2}$

I. $3\tfrac{5}{6} + 2\tfrac{4}{9}$

R. $\tfrac{3}{4} + 1\tfrac{8}{9}$

G. $5\frac{1}{9} + 5\frac{3}{7}$

T. $1\frac{6}{7} + \frac{1}{4}$

N. $7\frac{1}{3} + 2\frac{1}{4}$

B. $6\frac{8}{11} + 4\frac{1}{5}$

The French and Indian War (1754–1763) was fought between the English and French in North America. Both countries wanted to establish colonial dominance in the New World. After the war,

$$\overline{10\frac{34}{63}} \quad \overline{2\frac{23}{36}} \quad \overline{4\frac{1}{14}} \quad \overline{4\frac{1}{2}} \quad \overline{2\frac{3}{28}} \qquad \overline{10\frac{51}{55}} \quad \overline{2\frac{23}{36}} \quad \overline{6\frac{5}{18}} \quad \overline{2\frac{3}{28}} \quad \overline{4\frac{1}{2}} \quad \overline{6\frac{5}{18}} \quad \overline{9\frac{7}{12}}$$

gained all of Canada as part of the peace treaty of 1763.

EXERCISE
2·9

Add. Simplify, if necessary.

1. $2\frac{1}{3} + 1\frac{1}{2}$

2. $4\frac{1}{6} + 1\frac{1}{8}$

3. $4\frac{3}{5} + 2\frac{2}{10}$

4. $5\frac{6}{7} + \frac{1}{3}$

5. $2\frac{1}{6} + 3\frac{2}{9}$

6. $7\frac{3}{10} + 5\frac{2}{3}$

7. $5\frac{1}{4} + \frac{5}{16}$

8. $\frac{8}{9} + 3\frac{4}{5}$

9. $4\frac{2}{7} + 2\frac{3}{5}$

10. $2\frac{7}{11} + 2\frac{4}{5}$

11. $1\frac{3}{5} + 2\frac{5}{8}$

12. $11\frac{7}{12} + 3\frac{1}{4}$

13. $\frac{11}{12} + 3\frac{3}{4}$

14. $9\frac{2}{3} + 8\frac{4}{7}$

15. $4\frac{2}{3} + 8\frac{4}{7}$

16. $\frac{3}{7} + 12\frac{7}{9}$

Subtraction of fractions and mixed numbers (unlike denominators)

Subtracting fractions and mixed numbers with unlike denominators includes many of the same steps as adding fractions and mixed numbers. Follow these steps:

1. Rewrite the problem vertically, if necessary.

2. Find the least common denominator (LCD) of the fractions.

3. Write equivalent fractions. Leave the whole numbers as they are.

4. Subtract the second fraction from the first.

5. Subtract the second whole number from the first.

6. Write the difference in simplest form.

Example 1: $2\frac{1}{2} - 1\frac{1}{3}$

◆ Rewrite the problem vertically to create one column for the whole numbers and one column for the fractions.

$$2\frac{1}{2}$$
$$-\ 1\frac{1}{3}$$

◆ Find the LCD of the fractions. The LCD is 6.

◆ Write equivalent fractions. $2\frac{1}{2}$ is equivalent to $2\frac{3}{6}$. $1\frac{1}{3}$ is equivalent to $1\frac{2}{6}$.

◆ Rewrite the problem using equivalent fractions.

$$2\frac{3}{6}$$
$$-\ 1\frac{2}{6}$$

◆ Subtract the second numerator from the first numerator. The denominator remains the same.

$$2\frac{3}{6}$$
$$-\ 1\frac{2}{6}$$
$$\frac{1}{6}$$

◆ Subtract the whole numbers, 1 from 2.

$$2\frac{3}{6}$$
$$-\ 1\frac{2}{6}$$
$$1\frac{1}{6}$$

◆ $1\frac{1}{6}$ is the difference, which is in simplest form.

Example 2: $3\frac{3}{4} - \frac{2}{5}$

◆ Rewrite the problem vertically.

$$3\frac{3}{4}$$
$$-\ \frac{2}{5}$$

- Find the LCD of the fractions. The LCD is 20.

- Write equivalent fractions. $3\frac{3}{4}$ is equivalent to $3\frac{15}{20}$, and $\frac{2}{5}$ is equivalent to $\frac{8}{20}$.

- Rewrite the problem using the equivalent fractions.

$$3\frac{15}{20}$$
$$-\ \ \frac{8}{20}$$

- Subtract the second numerator from the first numerator. The denominator stays the same.

$$3\frac{15}{20}$$
$$-\ \ \frac{8}{20}$$
$$\overline{\quad\ \ \frac{7}{20}}$$

- Subtract the whole numbers, 0 from 3.

$$3\frac{15}{20}$$
$$-\ \ \frac{8}{20}$$
$$\overline{3\frac{7}{20}}$$

- $3\frac{7}{20}$ is the difference, which is in simplest form.

EXERCISE 2·10

Subtract. Simplify, if necessary. Write the letter of the problem in the space above its answer at the end of the exercise to complete the sentence. Some answers will be used more than once.

R. $3\frac{7}{8} - 1\frac{5}{16}$

O. $2\frac{9}{10} - \frac{3}{5}$

E. $4\frac{7}{9} - 3\frac{1}{6}$

I. $5\frac{6}{8} - 2\frac{2}{3}$

T. $6\frac{6}{12} - 4\frac{3}{8}$

P. $1\frac{4}{9} - \frac{2}{5}$

N. $4\frac{12}{21} - 3\frac{2}{7}$

S. $7\frac{8}{13} - 4\frac{3}{26}$

In the dictionary, an entry that is labeled "prep" is a

$\underline{\hspace{1.5em}}$ $\underline{\hspace{1.5em}}$ $\underline{\hspace{1.5em}}$ $\underline{\hspace{1.5em}}$ $\underline{\hspace{1.5em}}$ $\underline{\hspace{1.5em}}$ $\underline{\hspace{1.5em}}$ $\underline{\hspace{1.5em}}$ $\underline{\hspace{1.5em}}$ $\underline{\hspace{1.5em}}$ $\underline{\hspace{1.5em}}$

$1\frac{2}{45}$ $2\frac{9}{16}$ $1\frac{11}{18}$ $1\frac{2}{45}$ $2\frac{3}{10}$ $3\frac{1}{2}$ $3\frac{1}{12}$ $2\frac{1}{8}$ $3\frac{1}{12}$ $2\frac{3}{10}$ $1\frac{2}{7}$

EXERCISE 2·11

Subtract. Simplify, if necessary.

1. $2\frac{4}{5} - 1\frac{1}{2}$

2. $4\frac{5}{9} - 3\frac{1}{3}$

3. $4\frac{2}{7} - 3\frac{4}{21}$

4. $7\frac{5}{8} - 2\frac{1}{6}$

5. $6\frac{7}{8} - \frac{3}{4}$

6. $8\frac{7}{12} - 3\frac{3}{8}$

7. $8\frac{5}{6} - 3\frac{3}{4}$

8. $10\frac{4}{6} - 3\frac{2}{7}$

9. $1\frac{7}{8} - \frac{1}{3}$

10. $11\frac{4}{10} - 9\frac{2}{5}$

11. $4\frac{1}{2} - 2\frac{1}{5}$

12. $13\frac{5}{6} - 7\frac{3}{15}$

13. $9\frac{2}{3} - 7\frac{2}{5}$

14. $4\frac{4}{18} - 3\frac{1}{6}$

15. $10\frac{11}{15} - 6\frac{7}{10}$

16. $9\frac{12}{14} - \frac{5}{8}$

Subtraction of fractions and mixed numbers with renaming

Some subtraction problems require that you rename the mixed number before you can subtract the fractions. Follow the steps below.

1. Rewrite the problem vertically.

2. Find the least common denominator (LCD) of the fractions, if necessary, and write equivalent fractions.

3. Rewrite the first number in the subtraction problem by changing 1 whole to an equivalent fraction in which the denominator is equal to the LCD.

4. Add the whole to the fraction in the first number.

5. Subtract the second fraction from the first fraction. Subtract the whole numbers.

6. Write the difference in the simplest form.

Example 1: $3\frac{2}{3} - 1\frac{11}{12}$

◆ Rewrite the problem vertically.

$$3\tfrac{2}{3}$$
$$-\;1\tfrac{11}{12}$$

- ♦ Find the LCD of the fractions. The LCD is 12. $3\tfrac{2}{3}$ can be rewritten as $3\tfrac{8}{12}$. $1\tfrac{11}{12}$ remains the same.

- ♦ Rewrite the problem using equivalent fractions.

$$3\tfrac{8}{12}$$
$$-\;1\tfrac{11}{12}$$

- ♦ Because you cannot take the 11 away from the 8, you must rename the first mixed number. Write 1 whole as an equivalent fraction in which the denominator is the LCD. $1 = \tfrac{12}{12}$. Rename $3\tfrac{8}{12}$ as $\tfrac{12}{12} + 2\tfrac{8}{12}$ or $2\tfrac{20}{12}$.

- ♦ Rewrite the problem.

$$2\tfrac{20}{12}$$
$$-\;1\tfrac{11}{12}$$

- ♦ Subtract the second numerator from the first numerator. Subtract the whole numbers.

$$2\tfrac{20}{12}$$
$$-\;1\tfrac{11}{12}$$
$$1\tfrac{9}{12}$$

- ♦ The answer is $1\tfrac{9}{12}$, which is simplified to $1\tfrac{3}{4}$.

Example 2: $5\tfrac{1}{8} - 3\tfrac{3}{4}$

- ♦ Rewrite the problem vertically.

$$5\tfrac{1}{8}$$
$$-\;3\tfrac{3}{4}$$

- ♦ Find the LCD of the fractions. The LCD is 8. $3\tfrac{3}{4}$ is equivalent to $3\tfrac{6}{8}$. $5\tfrac{1}{8}$ stays the same.

- ♦ Rewrite the problem using equivalent fractions.

$$5\tfrac{1}{8}$$
$$-\;3\tfrac{6}{8}$$

- Because you cannot subtract 6 from 1, you must rename $5\frac{1}{8}$. Rename one whole as $\frac{8}{8}$ and add $\frac{8}{8}$ to $4\frac{1}{8}$ for a sum of $4\frac{9}{8}$.

- Rewrite the problem.

$$4\frac{9}{8}$$
$$-\ 3\frac{6}{8}$$

- Subtract the second numerator from the first numerator. Subtract the whole numbers.

$$4\frac{9}{8}$$
$$-\ 3\frac{6}{8}$$
$$\overline{1\frac{3}{8}}$$

- The answer is $1\frac{3}{8}$, which is in simplest form.

EXERCISE

2·12

Subtract. Simplify, if necessary. Write the letter of the problem in the space above its answer at the end of the exercise to complete the sentence. Some answers will be used more than once. Some answers will not be used.

M. $\quad 7\frac{1}{4} - 4\frac{2}{5}$

O. $\quad 6\frac{2}{3} - 2\frac{1}{8}$

E. $\quad 5\frac{2}{9} - 2\frac{1}{2}$

W. $\quad 7\frac{1}{4} - 3\frac{5}{6}$

A. $\quad 9\frac{5}{9} - 5\frac{1}{6}$

S. $\quad 5\frac{7}{10} - 3\frac{1}{2}$

J. $\quad 6\frac{3}{8} - 2\frac{4}{5}$

I. $\quad 8\frac{2}{6} - 4\frac{1}{4}$

D. $8 - 4\frac{4}{6}$

N. $7\frac{3}{4} - 5\frac{6}{7}$

___ $3\frac{23}{40}$ $4\frac{7}{18}$ $2\frac{17}{20}$ $2\frac{13}{18}$ $2\frac{1}{5}$ $2\frac{17}{20}$ $4\frac{7}{18}$ $3\frac{1}{3}$ $4\frac{1}{12}$ $2\frac{1}{5}$ $4\frac{13}{24}$ $1\frac{25}{28}$

is known as the "Father of our Constitution."

EXERCISE 2·13

Subtract. Simplify, if necessary.

1. $3\frac{2}{5} - 1\frac{3}{4}$

2. $3\frac{1}{2} - 1\frac{5}{6}$

3. $4\frac{1}{6} - 2\frac{1}{2}$

4. $8\frac{3}{10} - 3\frac{8}{15}$

5. $5\frac{3}{7} - 2\frac{3}{4}$

6. $8\frac{5}{8} - 7\frac{9}{10}$

7. $8\frac{5}{10} - 3\frac{3}{4}$

8. $10\frac{9}{14} - 3\frac{6}{7}$

9. $9\frac{1}{3} - 3\frac{5}{12}$

10. $15\frac{2}{11} - 8\frac{3}{5}$

11. $6 - 2\frac{1}{2}$

12. $4\frac{1}{12} - 2\frac{5}{8}$

13. $9\frac{3}{8} - 4\frac{7}{9}$

14. $8 - 3\frac{5}{9}$

15. $11\frac{2}{8} - 6\frac{4}{5}$

16. $10 - 1\frac{2}{5}$

Multiplication of fractions

Just as with multiplying whole numbers, multiplying fractions requires an understanding of basic multiplication facts. Follow these steps to multiply fractions.

1. Multiply the numerators.

2. Multiply the denominators.

3. Write the product in simplest form.

Example 1: $\frac{5}{6} \times \frac{2}{3}$

◆ Multiply the numerators.

◆ Multiply the denominators.

$$\frac{5}{6} \times \frac{2}{3} = \frac{10}{18}$$

◆ Write the product in simplest form. $\frac{10}{18} = \frac{5}{9}$

Example 2: $\frac{3}{4} \times \frac{2}{9}$

◆ Sometimes you may be able to use a shortcut and simplify fractions before you multiply. If you can find the greatest common factor (GCF) of any numerator and any denominator, you may divide each by the GCF. In this example, the GCF of the numerator 3 and the denominator 9 is 3. Divide both 3 and 9 by 3. Write the quotient as the new numerator and denominator. The GCF of the denominator 4 and the numerator 2 is 2. Divide both 4 and 2 by 2. Write the quotient as the new numerator and denominator. Then multiply the numerators and multiply the denominators.

$$\frac{3}{4} \times \frac{2}{9} = \frac{\overset{1}{\cancel{3}} \times \overset{1}{\cancel{2}}}{\underset{2}{\cancel{4}} \times \underset{3}{\cancel{9}}} = \frac{1}{6}$$

◆ $\frac{1}{6}$ is the product and is in simplest form. By using the shortcut, you eliminate the need to simplify your answer, provided you found the GCF. (If you found a common factor that was not the GCF and used the shortcut, you would have to simplify the product.) Notice that if you did not simplify before you multiplied, the product would still be the same. $\frac{3}{4} \times \frac{2}{9} = \frac{6}{36}$, which can be simplified to $\frac{1}{6}$.

EXERCISE
2·14

Multiply. Simplify, if necessary. Write the letter of the problem in the space above its answer at the end of the exercise to complete the sentence. Some answers will be used more than once.

Y. $\quad \frac{1}{3} \times \frac{4}{5}$

A. $\quad \frac{8}{10} \times \frac{4}{10}$

N. $\quad \frac{3}{8} \times \frac{1}{6}$

E. $\quad \frac{1}{2} \times \frac{2}{4}$

D. $\quad \frac{4}{9} \times \frac{2}{5}$

I. $\quad \frac{2}{5} \times \frac{7}{8}$

C. $\quad \frac{1}{8} \times \frac{1}{7}$

R. $\quad \frac{9}{12} \times \frac{24}{30}$

G. $\dfrac{12}{30} \times \dfrac{3}{10}$

L. $\dfrac{4}{12} \times \dfrac{3}{8}$

Thomas L. Jennings was the first African American to obtain a patent. He invented the

___ ___ ___ ‾ ___ ___ ___ ___ ___ ___ ___ ___ process.

$\dfrac{8}{45}$　$\dfrac{3}{5}$　$\dfrac{4}{15}$　$\dfrac{1}{56}$　$\dfrac{1}{8}$　$\dfrac{1}{4}$　$\dfrac{8}{25}$　$\dfrac{1}{16}$　$\dfrac{7}{20}$　$\dfrac{1}{16}$　$\dfrac{3}{25}$

EXERCISE 2·15

Multiply. Simplify, if necessary.

1. $\dfrac{4}{5} \times \dfrac{2}{7}$

2. $\dfrac{5}{8} \times \dfrac{4}{10}$

3. $\dfrac{5}{6} \times \dfrac{2}{5}$

4. $\dfrac{2}{7} \times \dfrac{7}{9}$

5. $\dfrac{7}{8} \times \dfrac{2}{3}$

6. $\dfrac{3}{9} \times \dfrac{4}{12}$

7. $\dfrac{1}{3} \times \dfrac{7}{8}$

8. $\dfrac{4}{8} \times \dfrac{9}{11}$

9. $\frac{1}{2} \times \frac{6}{7}$

10. $\frac{20}{25} \times \frac{5}{10}$

11. $\frac{4}{20} \times \frac{5}{8}$

12. $\frac{18}{21} \times \frac{7}{9}$

13. $\frac{5}{12} \times \frac{18}{20}$

14. $\frac{3}{16} \times \frac{8}{15}$

15. $\frac{5}{11} \times \frac{4}{10}$

16. $\frac{9}{30} \times \frac{5}{18}$

Multiplication of fractions, mixed numbers, and whole numbers

The procedure for multiplying fractions and mixed numbers is similar to multiplying fractions. But you must first change mixed numbers or whole numbers to improper fractions. Follow these steps:

1. Write mixed numbers or whole numbers as improper fractions. (Remember, whole numbers can be written as an improper fraction by placing the number over 1.)

2. Use the shortcut if any numerator and denominator have a common factor.

3. Multiply the numerators.

4. Multiply the denominators.

5. Write the product in simplest form.

Example 1: $\frac{2}{9} \times 1\frac{1}{2}$

♦ Change $1\frac{1}{2}$ to an improper fraction. $1\frac{1}{2} = \frac{3}{2}$

- Rewrite the problem.

  $\frac{2}{9} \times \frac{3}{2}$

- Use the shortcut. Then multiply the numerators and multiply the denominators.

  $\frac{\overset{1}{\cancel{2}}}{\underset{3}{\cancel{9}}} \times \frac{\overset{1}{\cancel{3}}}{\underset{1}{\cancel{2}}} = \frac{1}{3}$

- The product is $\frac{1}{3}$, which is in simplest form.

Example 2: $3\frac{1}{3} \times 2\frac{1}{4}$

- Change both mixed numbers to improper fractions. $3\frac{1}{3} = \frac{10}{3}$ and $2\frac{1}{4} = \frac{9}{4}$

- Rewrite the problem.

  $\frac{10}{3} \times \frac{9}{4}$

- Use the shortcut. Then multiply the numerators and multiply the denominators.

  $\frac{\overset{5}{\cancel{10}} \times \overset{3}{\cancel{9}}}{\underset{1}{\cancel{3}} \times \underset{2}{\cancel{4}}} = \frac{15}{2} = 7\frac{1}{2}$

- $7\frac{1}{2}$ is the simplified product.

Multiply. Simplify, if necessary. Write the letter of the problem in the space above its answer at the end of the exercise to complete the sentence. Some answers will be used more than once.

R. $\frac{3}{5} \times 1\frac{1}{5}$

B. $4\frac{1}{2} \times 1\frac{7}{8}$

I. $\frac{2}{8} \times 1\frac{2}{3}$

A. $\frac{2}{5} \times 6$

E. $1\frac{1}{2} \times \frac{4}{5}$

G. $1\frac{2}{3} \times 1\frac{3}{5}$

D. $\frac{6}{10} \times 3\frac{1}{3}$

T. $4\frac{3}{5} \times 2$

M. $1\frac{1}{2} \times 1\frac{1}{2}$

S. $8\frac{3}{4} \times 1\frac{1}{4}$

In 1969, the first episode of

$\underline{\quad}$ $\underline{\quad}$ $\underline{\quad}$ $\underline{\quad}$ $\underline{\quad}$ $\underline{\quad}$ $\qquad$ $\underline{\quad}$ $\underline{\quad}$ $\underline{\quad}$ $\underline{\quad}$ $\underline{\quad}$ $\underline{\quad}$ introduced

$10\frac{15}{16}$ $\;1\frac{1}{5}\;$ $10\frac{15}{16}$ $\;2\frac{2}{5}\;$ $\;2\frac{1}{4}\;$ $\;1\frac{1}{5}\;$ $\qquad$ $10\frac{15}{16}$ $\;9\frac{1}{5}\;$ $\;\frac{18}{25}\;$ $\;1\frac{1}{5}\;$ $\;1\frac{1}{5}\;$ $\;9\frac{1}{5}\;$

$\underline{\quad}$ $\underline{\quad}$ $\underline{\quad}$ $\qquad$ $\underline{\quad}$ $\underline{\quad}$ $\underline{\quad}$ $\underline{\quad}$ to a generation of kids and adults.

$8\frac{7}{16}$ $\;\frac{5}{12}\;$ $\;2\frac{2}{3}\;$ $\qquad$ $8\frac{7}{16}$ $\;\frac{5}{12}\;$ $\;\frac{18}{25}\;$ $\;2\;$

EXERCISE
2·17

Multiply. Simplify, if necessary.

1. $\frac{3}{4} \times 1\frac{2}{3}$

2. $2\frac{5}{7} \times 3\frac{1}{2}$

3. $\frac{5}{9} \times 4\frac{3}{4}$

4. $4\frac{1}{5} \times 2\frac{3}{7}$

5. $\frac{8}{10} \times 1\frac{1}{2}$

6. $8 \times \frac{3}{4}$

7. $6\frac{5}{7} \times 7\frac{1}{6}$

8. $\dfrac{7}{9} \times 3\dfrac{3}{5}$

9. $2\dfrac{4}{5} \times 4\dfrac{4}{6}$

10. $1\dfrac{1}{11} \times 2\dfrac{3}{4}$

11. $\dfrac{7}{8} \times 5$

12. $3\dfrac{4}{12} \times 2\dfrac{2}{6}$

13. $3\dfrac{1}{2} \times 3$

14. $10\dfrac{1}{5} \times 6\dfrac{1}{3}$

15. $6\dfrac{1}{5} \times 2\dfrac{2}{3}$

16. $9\dfrac{3}{8} \times 4\dfrac{4}{5}$

Division of fractions

Dividing fractions requires the use of multiplication and the reciprocal of the divisor. Follow these steps:

1. Rewrite the division problem as a multiplication problem by writing the reciprocal of the divisor and changing the division sign to a multiplication sign.

   ◆ To write the reciprocal of the divisor, write a new fraction by switching the numerator and the denominator.

   ◆ For example, the reciprocal of $\dfrac{4}{5}$ is $\dfrac{5}{4}$.

2. Multiply the fractions to find the product. Use the shortcut, if possible.

3. Write the product in simplest form.

Example 1: $\frac{3}{4} \times \frac{2}{1}$

- Rewrite the problem by writing the reciprocal of the divisor and changing the division sign to a multiplication sign.

$$\frac{3}{4} \times \frac{2}{1}$$

- Use the shortcut. Then multiply the numerators and multiply the denominators. Write the product in simplest form.

$$\frac{3}{\cancel{4}_2} \times \frac{\cancel{2}^1}{1} = \frac{3}{2} = 1\frac{1}{2}$$

- $1\frac{1}{2}$ is the simplified product.

Example 2: $\frac{3}{8} \div \frac{3}{4}$

- Rewrite the problem by writing the reciprocal of the divisor and changing the division sign to a multiplication sign.

$$\frac{3}{8} \times \frac{4}{3}$$

- Use the shortcut. Then multiply the numerators and multiply the denominators.

$$\frac{{}^1\cancel{3}}{{}_2\cancel{8}} \times \frac{\cancel{4}^1}{\cancel{3}_1} = \frac{1}{2}$$

- $\frac{1}{2}$ is the simplified product.

EXERCISE

2·18

Divide. Simplify, if necessary. Write the letter of the problem in the space above its answer at the end of the exercise to complete the sentence. Some answers will not be used. Some answers will be used more than once.

M. $\quad \frac{10}{11} \div \frac{2}{5}$

A. $\quad \frac{12}{30} \div \frac{3}{4}$

K. $\quad \frac{7}{10} \div \frac{3}{4}$

R. $\quad \frac{3}{8} \div \frac{4}{10}$

S. $\quad \frac{2}{8} \div \frac{1}{6}$

E. $\quad \frac{4}{5} \div \frac{8}{9}$

N. $\dfrac{1}{5} \div \dfrac{3}{4}$

D. $\dfrac{1}{9} \div \dfrac{5}{10}$

$\overline{}$ $\overline{}$ $\overline{}$ $\overline{}$ $\overline{}$ $\overline{}$ $\overline{}$ $\overline{}$ —— were invented in 1917 and were

$1\frac{1}{2}$ $\frac{4}{5}$ $\frac{9}{10}$ $\frac{8}{15}$ $\frac{14}{15}$ $\frac{9}{10}$ $\frac{15}{16}$ $1\frac{1}{2}$

known as $\overline{}$ $\overline{}$ $\overline{}$ $\overline{}$.

$\frac{14}{15}$ $\frac{9}{10}$ $\frac{2}{9}$ $1\frac{1}{2}$

EXERCISE
2·19

Divide. Simplify, if necessary.

1. $\dfrac{2}{7} \div \dfrac{4}{5}$

2. $\dfrac{3}{5} \div \dfrac{7}{10}$

3. $\dfrac{5}{6} \div \dfrac{1}{3}$

4. $\dfrac{4}{9} \div \dfrac{2}{12}$

5. $\dfrac{8}{9} \div \dfrac{7}{8}$

6. $\dfrac{11}{12} \div \dfrac{22}{25}$

7. $\dfrac{2}{3} \div \dfrac{4}{5}$

8. $\dfrac{3}{8} \div \dfrac{3}{8}$

9. $\dfrac{3}{5} \div \dfrac{1}{8}$

10. $\dfrac{3}{4} \div \dfrac{1}{4}$

11. $\dfrac{3}{4} \div \dfrac{1}{6}$

12. $\dfrac{13}{14} \div \dfrac{3}{7}$

13. $\dfrac{1}{10} \div \dfrac{5}{6}$

14. $\dfrac{14}{15} \div \dfrac{3}{5}$

15. $\dfrac{14}{20} \div \dfrac{7}{10}$

16. $\dfrac{6}{11} \div \dfrac{2}{8}$

Division of fractions, mixed numbers, and whole numbers

The process for dividing fractions and mixed numbers is similar to the process for dividing fractions. Follow these steps to divide fractions and mixed numbers.

1. Write mixed numbers and whole numbers as improper fractions.

2. Rewrite the division problem as a multiplication problem by writing the reciprocal of the divisor and changing the division sign to a multiplication sign.

3. Use the shortcut, if possible. Then multiply the numerators and multiply the denominators.

4. Simplify your answer, if necessary.

Example 1: $2\dfrac{1}{2} \div \dfrac{3}{4}$

◆ Change $2\dfrac{1}{2}$ to an improper fraction. $2\dfrac{1}{2} = \dfrac{5}{2}$

- Rewrite the problem by writing the reciprocal of the divisor and changing the division sign to a multiplication sign.

$$\frac{5}{2} \times \frac{4}{3}$$

- Use the shortcut. Then multiply the numerators and multiply the denominators. Simplify, if needed.

$$\frac{5}{\cancel{2}_1} \times \frac{\cancel{4}^2}{3} = \frac{10}{3} = 3\frac{1}{3}$$

- $3\frac{1}{3}$ is in simplest form.

Example 2: $3\frac{1}{4} \div 5\frac{1}{5}$

- Change both mixed numbers to improper fractions. $3\frac{1}{4} = \frac{13}{4}$ and $5\frac{1}{5} = \frac{26}{5}$

- Rewrite the problem by writing the reciprocal of the divisor and changing the division sign to a multiplication sign.

$$\frac{13}{4} \times \frac{5}{26}$$

- Use the shortcut. Then multiply the numerators and multiply the denominators.

$$\frac{\cancel{13}^1}{4} \times \frac{5}{\cancel{26}_2} = \frac{5}{8}$$

- $\frac{5}{8}$ is in simplest form.

EXERCISE

2·20

Divide. Simplify, if necessary. Write the letter of the problem in the space above its answer at the end of the exercise to complete the sentence. Some answers will be used more than once.

I. $2\frac{1}{2} \div 2\frac{1}{2}$

A. $\frac{6}{10} \div 4\frac{1}{2}$

S. $3\frac{2}{3} \div 1\frac{1}{2}$

N. $4\frac{1}{2} \div \frac{1}{5}$

D. $8 \div \frac{1}{4}$

O. $2\frac{1}{3} \div 3$

F. $\frac{3}{7} \div 3$

L. $7 \div 2\frac{1}{8}$

The name of the state ── ── ── ── ── ── ── means
                            1   $22\frac{1}{2}$ 32   1 $\frac{2}{15}$ $22\frac{1}{2}$ $\frac{2}{15}$

── ── ── ──   ── ──   ── ── ── ── ── ── ── .
$3\frac{5}{17}$ $\frac{2}{15}$ $22\frac{1}{2}$ 32 $\frac{7}{9}$ $\frac{1}{7}$ 1 $22\frac{1}{2}$ 32   1 $\frac{2}{15}$ $22\frac{1}{2}$ 2 $\frac{4}{9}$

EXERCISE 2·21

Divide. Simplify, if necessary.

1. $3 \div \frac{4}{5}$

2. $3\frac{2}{3} \div 4\frac{1}{4}$

3. $2\frac{1}{3} \div 1\frac{5}{7}$

4. $1\frac{1}{8} \div 5\frac{3}{4}$

5. $4\frac{1}{2} \div \frac{1}{2}$

6. $6\frac{7}{8} \div 4$

7. $2\frac{6}{8} \div 2\frac{2}{3}$

8. $4\frac{2}{7} \div \frac{3}{14}$

9. $\frac{5}{9} \div 2$

10. $12\frac{5}{12} \div 2\frac{1}{6}$

11. $6\frac{3}{4} \div 2\frac{1}{3}$

12. $10\frac{2}{9} \div 5\frac{1}{3}$

13. $9 \div \frac{3}{7}$

14. $8 \div 2\frac{2}{5}$

15. $2 \div \frac{1}{6}$

16. $7\frac{9}{10} \div 3\frac{1}{6}$

EXERCISE 2·22

Perform the indicated operation. Simplify, if necessary.

1. $4\frac{1}{10} + 5\frac{3}{4}$

2. $3\frac{1}{5} - 1\frac{2}{3}$

3. $\frac{2}{3} + \frac{1}{3}$

4. $6\frac{7}{8} \div 2\frac{1}{4}$

5. $5\frac{4}{5} \div 2$

6. $\frac{9}{10} + \frac{3}{4}$

7. $2\frac{5}{7} - \frac{1}{3}$

8. $5\frac{2}{7} \times \frac{5}{12}$

9. $\frac{5}{6} \times \frac{7}{10}$

10. $4\frac{3}{7} - 1\frac{1}{7}$

11. $\frac{7}{8} \div \frac{3}{5}$

12. $\frac{5}{6} + 3\frac{2}{5}$

13. $\frac{8}{12} - \frac{5}{8}$

14. $9\frac{1}{9} \div \frac{5}{6}$

15. $4\frac{1}{6} \times 2$

16. $\frac{5}{11} \times \frac{9}{20}$

Connecting fractions and decimals

Place value

In our base 10 number system, the value of a digit is determined by its place. The value of a place is 10 times the value of the place to its right. The following graphic organizer shows the base 10 number system for whole numbers through hundred millions. The smallest place value on this chart is the ones place. The tens place is 10 times larger than the ones place. The hundreds place is 10 times larger than the tens place, and so on.

Hundred millions	Ten millions	Millions	Hundred thousands	Ten thousands	Thousands	Hundreds	Tens	Ones

For example, the number 234 equals 2 hundreds, 3 tens, and 4 ones. This number is read "two hundred thirty-four." The number 32,904 equals 3 ten thousands, 2 thousands, 9 hundreds, 0 tens, and 4 ones. It is read "thirty-two thousand, nine hundred four."

The place value to the right of a decimal point represents numbers that are less than 1. These numbers are called decimals. Each place value still represents 10 times the place value of the number to its right. Conversely, each place value to the right is $\frac{1}{10}$ of the place value to its left. The following figure is a graphic organizer for base 10 numbers that are 1 and less, through hundred-millionths. The decimal point is placed after the ones place.

Ones	Tenths	Hundredths	Thousandths	Ten-thousandths	Hundred-thousandths	Millionths	Ten-millionths	Hundred-millionths

For example, the number 0.45 equals 0 ones, 4 tenths, and 5 hundredths. It is read "forty-five hundredths." Zeros are used to hold a place when no number is in that place. The number 5.026 equals 5 ones, 0 tenths, 2 hundredths, and 6 thousandths. It is read "five and twenty-six thousandths." The "and" represents the decimal point.

Example 1: Find the value of the underlined digit: 321.<u>6</u>8

- ◆ The 6 is underlined and represents the first place to the right of the decimal point. This is the tenths place. The 6 represents 6 tenths.

Example 2: Write 0.295 in words.

- ◆ There are 2 tenths, 9 hundredths, and 5 thousandths. This number, written in words, is "two hundred ninety-five thousandths."

Example 3: Write seventy-three hundredths in standard form.

- ◆ Standard form is the way numbers are usually written, with a digit from 0 to 9 in each place.
- ◆ Because this number ends in "-ths" the digits must be written to the right of the decimal point.
- ◆ Write the numbers in their appropriate place. Seventy-three hundredths is written as 0.73.

EXERCISE 3·1

Write the value of the underlined digit.

1. 34.<u>8</u>91

2. 0.6718<u>2</u>

3. <u>4</u>5.91

4. 9.1<u>05</u>

Write each decimal in words.

5. 1.85

6. 0.402

7. 12.3

8. 1.034

Write each value in standard form.

9. three and five tenths

10. eleven and seventy-five hundredths

11. three hundred forty-five thousandths

12. seven ten-thousandths

Powers of 10

Place value in our number system is based on powers of 10. Each place is 10 times larger than the place to its right. Similarly, each place is $\frac{1}{10}$ of the place to its left. The increases and decreases in value between the places can be expressed as powers of 10.

A power is also called an exponent. An exponent tells how many times the base is multiplied by itself. For example, in 2^3, 2 is the base and 3 is the exponent. 2^3 means that 2 is multiplied by itself 3 times. $2^3 = 2 \times 2 \times 2 = 8$. Note that 2^3 does *not* mean 2×3.

Each place value can be expressed as a power of 10 as shown on the following chart.

10^8	10^7	10^6	10^5	10^4	10^3	10^2	10^1	10^0
Hundred millions	Ten millions	Millions	Hundred thousands	Ten thousands	Thousands	Hundreds	Tens	Ones

Here are some examples of powers of 10.

$10^0 = 1$ 10 to the zero power represents the ones place.

$10^1 = 10$ 10 to the first power represents the tens place.

$10^2 = 10 \times 10 = 100$ 10 to the second power represents the hundreds place. This pattern continues with each consecutive place value.

The place value of the digits to the right of a decimal point can also be expressed as powers of 10 as shown on the following chart. Negative exponents are used to show the powers of 10 that are less than 1.

10^0	10^{-1}	10^{-2}	10^{-3}	10^{-4}	10^{-5}	10^{-6}	10^{-7}	10^{-8}
Ones	Tenths	Hundredths	Thousandths	Ten-thousandths	Hundred-thousandths	Millionths	Ten-millionths	Hundred-millionths nes

Here are some examples of powers of 10 that are less than 1.

$10^{-1} = \frac{1}{10} = 0.1$ 10^{-1} is read "ten to the negative first power." This power of 10 represents the tenths place.

$10^{-2} = \frac{1}{10 \times 10} = \frac{1}{100} = 0.01$ 10^{-2} is read "ten to the negative second power." This power of 10 represents the hundredths place.

$10^{-3} = \frac{1}{10 \times 10 \times 10} = \frac{1}{1000} = 0.001$ 10^{-3} is read "ten to the negative third power." This power of 10 represents the thousandths place.

EXERCISE

3·2

Write a multiplication sentence for each expression. Then find the value of each expression.

1. 10^2

2. 10^1

3. 10^4

4. 10^{-2}

5. 10^{-3}

6. 10^{3}

7. 10^{-1}

8. 10^{5}

9. 10^{-6}

10. 10^{6}

11. 10^{10}

12. 10^{-8}

13. 10^{0}

14. 10^{-4}

15. 10^{7}

16. 10^{-10}

Expanded form and standard form

The value of a digit depends on its place in the number. Every number can be written as the sum of the values of its digits. To write numbers in expanded form, find the place value of each digit. Then write an addition statement.

Example 1: Write 45.3 in expanded form.

- ◆ Find the value of each digit. There are 4 tens, 5 ones, and 3 tenths.
- ◆ Rewrite the number as a sum of the digits' place values. 45.3 = 40 + 5 + 0.3

Example 2: Write 0.872 in expanded form.

- ◆ Find the value of each digit. There are 8 tenths, 7 hundredths, and 2 thousandths.
- ◆ Rewrite the number as a sum of the digits' place values. 0.872 = 0.8 + 0.07 + 0.002

You can also write a number that is in expanded form in standard form.

Example 1: Write 6 + 0.4 + 0.03 in standard form.

- ◆ Find the value of each digit. There are 6 ones, 4 tenths, and 3 hundredths.
- ◆ Write each digit in its correct place to write the number in standard form. 6.43

Example 2: Write 50 + 6 + 0.2 + 0.001 in standard form.

- ◆ Find the value of each digit. There are 5 tens, 6 ones, 2 tenths, 0 hundredths, and 1 thousandth.
- ◆ Write each digit in its correct place to write the number in standard form. 56.201

EXERCISE
3·3

Write each number in expanded form.

1. 43.84

2. 5.92

3. 501.9

4. 7.821

5. 9.349

6. 0.1975

7. 12.983

8. 104.98

Write each number in standard form.

9. 9 + 0.3 + 0.005

10. 0.1 + 0.04 + 0.005

11. 10 + 3 + 0.006

12. 60 + 7 + 0.4 + 0.009

13. 100 + 70 + 4 + 0.02

14. 300 + 9 + 0.8 + 0.04

15. 90 + 0.006

16. 200 + 40 + 0.08 + 0.008

Writing fractions and mixed numbers as decimals

Every fraction can be written as an equivalent decimal or whole number. Fractions that have a denominator that is a power of 10, such as 10, 100, and 1,000, are the easiest to convert to decimals.

Example 1: Write $\frac{9}{10}$ as a decimal.

- ◆ Because the denominator of the fraction is 10, the numerator is written in the tenths place of the decimal. $\frac{9}{10} = 0.9$

Example 2: Write $\frac{87}{100}$ as a decimal.

- ◆ Because the denominator of the fraction is 100, the numerator is written in the hundredths place of the decimal. $\frac{87}{100} = 0.87$

Some fractions whose denominators are not powers of 10 can be written as equivalent fractions whose denominators are powers of 10.

Example 1: Write $\frac{3}{4}$ as a decimal.

- ◆ The denominator can be multiplied by 25 to equal 100.
- ◆ Use this information to write an equivalent fraction with a denominator of 100.

$$\frac{3}{4} = \frac{3 \times 25}{4 \times 25} = \frac{75}{100}$$

- ◆ The denominator, 100, represents the hundredths place. $\frac{3}{4} = \frac{75}{100} = 0.75$

Example 2: Write $\frac{5}{8}$ as a decimal.

- ◆ The denominator can be multiplied by 125 to equal 1,000.
- ◆ Write an equivalent fraction with a denominator of 1,000. $\frac{5}{8} = \frac{5 \times 125}{8 \times 125} = \frac{625}{1000}$
- ◆ The denominator, 1,000, represents the thousandths place. $\frac{5}{8} = \frac{625}{1000} = 0.625$

If the denominator of the fraction is not or cannot be multiplied to a power of 10, follow these steps:

1. Write a division problem and divide the numerator by the denominator.

2. Add a decimal point after the number in the dividend and add one zero.

3. Divide. (You may have to add more zeros in the dividend.)

4. Continue dividing until the remainder is zero or until a digit or group of digits repeats.

5. If a digit or group of digits repeat, place a bar over the digit or digits that repeat.

Example 1: Write $\frac{5}{6}$ as a decimal.

- ◆ Divide the numerator by the denominator. Place a decimal point after the 5. Add a zero in the dividend.

$$\begin{array}{r} 0.8 \\ 6\overline{)5.0} \\ \underline{48} \\ 2 \end{array}$$

- Since the remainder is 2, add another 0 in the dividend. Continue to divide.

$$\begin{array}{r} 0.83 \\ 6\overline{)5.00} \\ \underline{48} \\ 20 \\ \underline{18} \\ 2 \end{array}$$

- Again the remainder is 2. If you add another 0 in the dividend and continue to divide, the remainder will be 2. $\frac{5}{6}$ is equivalent to a repeating decimal. (A repeating decimal contains a digit or a group of digits that repeats forever in the same order.)

- Draw a line over the digit or group of digits that repeats. This line is called the repetend and shows that the digit or digits beneath it repeat.

- $\frac{5}{6} = 0.8\overline{3}$ The line over the 3 indicates that the 3 repeats forever.

The steps for converting mixed numbers to decimals are the same as converting fractions to decimals. Leave the whole number as it is and write the fraction as a decimal.

Example 1: $3\frac{2}{5}$

- 3 is the whole number and does not change. The denominator, 5, can be multiplied by 2 to make an equivalent fraction whose denominator is 10.

$$\frac{2}{5} = \frac{2 \times 2}{5 \times 2} = \frac{4}{10}$$

- $\frac{4}{10} = 0.4$ Include the whole number for an answer of 3.4.

Example 2: $2\frac{1}{9}$

- 2 is the whole number and does not change.

- Because the denominator, 9, cannot be multiplied to make an equivalent fraction whose denominator is a power of 10, divide the numerator by the denominator. $1 \div 9$

- Place a decimal point after the 1 and add one zero. Divide. Because there is a remainder of 1, add another zero and divide.

$$\begin{array}{r} 0.11 \\ 9\overline{)1.00} \\ \underline{9} \\ 10 \\ \underline{9} \\ 1 \end{array}$$

- But each time you divide, the remainder will be 1. $\frac{1}{9}$ is a repeating decimal. $\frac{1}{9} = 0.\overline{1}$

- Include the whole number. $2\frac{1}{9} = 2.\overline{1}$

Write each fraction as an equivalent decimal. Write the letter of the problem in the space above its answer at the end of the exercise to complete the sentence. One answer will be used twice. Some answers will not be used.

E. $\dfrac{1}{4}$

D. $5\dfrac{1}{2}$

O. $\dfrac{2}{20}$

S. $\dfrac{7}{8}$

I. $3\dfrac{2}{3}$

M. $\dfrac{1}{6}$

K. $\dfrac{8}{15}$

Z. $\dfrac{4}{9}$

T. $3\dfrac{4}{50}$

N. $\dfrac{11}{12}$

There are 24 \underline{} \underline{} \underline{} \underline{} \qquad \underline{} \underline{} \underline{} \underline{} \underline{}

3.08   3.$\overline{6}$ 0.1$\overline{6}$ 0.25   0.$\overline{4}$ 0.1   0.91$\overline{6}$ 0.25   0.875

around the world. Each has a longitude of 15°.

Write each fraction or mixed number as a decimal.

1. $\dfrac{5}{8}$

2. $\dfrac{9}{15}$

3. $3\dfrac{2}{5}$

4. $\dfrac{2}{3}$

5. $\dfrac{3}{10}$

6. $7\dfrac{9}{16}$

7. $2\dfrac{3}{4}$

8. $\dfrac{3}{20}$

9. $5\dfrac{1}{6}$

10. $\dfrac{5}{25}$

11. $\dfrac{2}{9}$

12. $\dfrac{14}{30}$

13. $6\dfrac{8}{11}$

14. $\frac{7}{11}$

15. $8\frac{1}{12}$

16. $4\frac{11}{16}$

Writing decimals as fractions or mixed numbers

Every terminating and every repeating decimal can be converted to a fraction. To convert a decimal to a fraction you must first find the decimal's place value.

Example 1: Write 0.42 as a fraction.

- ◆ 0.42 is 42 hundredths. Because the place value is hundredths, the denominator of the fraction is 100.

- ◆ Write the numbers to the right of the decimal point in the numerator of the fraction. Write the place value as the denominator. $\frac{42}{100}$

- ◆ Write the fraction in simplest form. $\frac{42}{100} = \frac{42 \div 2}{100 \div 2} = \frac{21}{50}$

- ◆ 0.42 = $\frac{21}{50}$.

Example 2: Write 0.812 as a fraction.

- ◆ 0.812 is 8 hundred 12 thousandths.

- ◆ Write 812 in the numerator and 1,000 in the denominator. $\frac{812}{1000}$

- ◆ Write the fraction in simplest form. $\frac{812}{1000} = \frac{812 \div 4}{1000 \div 4} = \frac{203}{250}$

- ◆ 0.812 = $\frac{203}{250}$

A repeating decimal is a decimal that has a digit or a group of digits that repeats. For example, $0.\overline{2}$ can be rewritten as 0.222 . . . , and $0.\overline{16}$ can be rewritten as 0.16161616 . . . .

You can write repeating decimals as fractions by following these steps:

1. Write the decimal over 1.

2. Multiply the decimal by 1.

- If one digit repeats, express 1 as $\frac{10-1}{9}$.
- If two digits repeat, express 1 as $\frac{100-1}{99}$ and so on.

3. Use the distributive property to simplify the numerator.

4. Write the fraction in simplest form.

Example: Write $0.\overline{7}$ as a fraction.

- Write $0.\overline{7}$ over 1. $\frac{0.\overline{7}}{1}$

- Because only one digit repeats, multiply by 1, expressed as $\frac{10-1}{9}$. $\frac{0.\overline{7}}{1} \times \frac{(10-1)}{9}$

- Use the distributive property by multiplying $0.\overline{7} \times 10$ and $0.\overline{7} \times 1$. Simplify the numerator by subtracting $0.\overline{7}$ from $7.\overline{7}$. $\frac{0.\overline{7}}{1} \times \frac{(10-1)}{9} = \frac{0.\overline{7} \times 10 - 0.\overline{7} \times 1}{9} = \frac{7.\overline{7} - 0.\overline{7}}{9} = \frac{7}{9}$

- $\frac{7}{9}$ is the answer, expressed in simplest form.

Mixed numbers can also be converted to decimals, following a procedure similar to changing terminating and repeating decimals to fractions.

Example 1: Write 2.5 as a mixed number.

- The whole number 2 does not change.

- Because 2.5 is 2 and 5 tenths, the numerator of the fraction is 5 and the denominator of the fraction is 10. Write $\frac{5}{10}$.

- Write the fraction in simplest form. $\frac{5}{10} = \frac{5 \div 5}{10 \div 5} = \frac{1}{2}$

- Combine the whole number with the simplified fraction. $2.5 = 2\frac{1}{2}$

Example 2: Express $8.\overline{25}$ as a mixed number.

- The whole number 8 does not change.

- Write $0.\overline{25}$ over 1 and multiply by $\frac{100-1}{99}$ because 2 digits repeat. $\frac{0.\overline{25}}{1} \times \frac{(100-1)}{99}$

- Use the distributive property and simplify the numerator.

$\frac{0.\overline{25}}{1} \times \frac{(100-1)}{99} = \frac{0.\overline{25} \times 100 - 0.\overline{25} \times 1}{99} = \frac{25.\overline{25} - 0.\overline{25}}{99} = \frac{25}{99}$

- $\frac{25}{99}$ is in simplest form.

- Combine the whole number and the simplified fraction. $8.\overline{25} = 8\frac{25}{99}$

Write each decimal as an equivalent fraction or mixed number. Write the letter of the problem in the space above its answer at the end of the exercise to complete the sentence. Some answers will be used twice. Some answers will not be used.

U. 0.9

I. 1.34

S. 0.35

N. 2.25

E. 0.125

O. 4.89

C. $0.\overline{12}$

H. $0.\overline{5}$

R. 4.95

A. 0.8

| $\frac{5}{9}$ | $\frac{9}{10}$ | $4\frac{19}{20}$ | $4\frac{19}{20}$ | $1\frac{17}{50}$ | $\frac{4}{33}$ | $\frac{4}{5}$ | $2\frac{1}{4}$ | $\frac{1}{8}$ | $\frac{7}{20}$ |

gain strength from warm tropical air over the ocean.

Write each decimal as a fraction or mixed number.

1. 0.75

2. 1.55

3. $0.\overline{83}$

4. 0.955

5. 1.4

6. $3.\overline{5}$

7. 3.92

8. 0.48

9. 0.515

10. 5.15

11. 0.625

12. 0.2

13. $2.\overline{8}$

14. 2.192

15. 0.$\overline{09}$

16. 1.$\overline{46}$

Decimals on the number line

Every decimal can be represented as a point on a number line. To graph decimals on a number line, first determine the number of units you will use to divide the number line.

Example 1: Place 0.6 on a number line.

- ◆ Because the decimal is tenths, divide the number line into tenths, using small lines called tick marks.

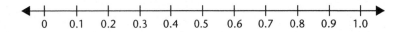

- ◆ Count 6 tick marks from zero. This tick mark represents 0.6. Place a point on the tick mark to show 0.6.

Example 2: Place 1.55 on a number line.

- ◆ Although 1.55 represents hundredths, you do not need to divide the number line into hundredths. Instead place tick marks between 1.5 and 1.6, dividing the number line into 10 equally spaced intervals.

- ◆ Start at 1.5. Count 5 tick marks to the right. This tick mark represents 1.55. Place a point on the tick mark to show 1.55.

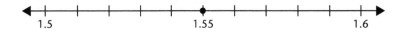

Write the decimal represented on each number line.

1.

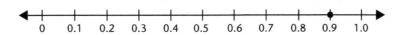

2.

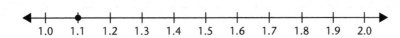

3.

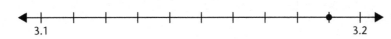

4.

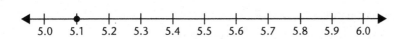

5.

6.

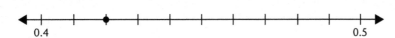

Draw a number line for each problem. Then place each decimal on the number line.

7. 0.3

8. 1.88

9. 0.8

10. 1.25

11. 0.67

12. 2.34

13. 0.732

14. 5.7 and 4.9

15. 1.5 and 2.01

16. 0.851 and 0.99

Comparing decimals

Comparing decimals is similar to comparing whole numbers. If two decimals have the same place value, the higher number is larger. But if decimals have different place values, you must compare the numbers according to each place.

Using a number line is one way to compare decimals.

Example 1: Compare 0.7 and 0.9 using <, >, or =.

- ◆ Both 7 and 9 are in the tenths place.

- ◆ Because 9 is larger than 7, 0.9 > 0.7 or 0.7 < 0.9. This can be shown on the number line that follows.

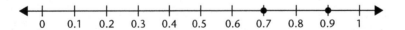

- ◆ 0.9 is farther to the right on the number line and is the larger number. (Remember that a number located to the right of another number on a number line has the larger value.)

Example 2: Compare 0.82 and 0.64 using <, >, or =.

- ◆ Both numbers are in the hundredths place. Because 82 is larger than 64, 0.82 > 0.64 or 0.64 < 0.82.

Example 3: Compare 1.304 and 1.3025 using <, >, or =.

- ◆ 1.304 ends in the thousandths place, but 1.3025 ends in the ten-thousandths place. To find which is the larger number, begin at the left-most digit. In this example, 1 is the left-most digit in both numbers. Because each 1 is in the ones place, consider the next digit. 3 is in the tenths place in both numbers. 0 is in the hundredths place for both numbers. 4 is in the thousandths place in 1.304, but 2 is in the thousandths place in 1.3025. 4 is larger than 2. Therefore, 1.304 > 1.3025.

◆ Notice that more digits do not necessarily mean a larger number. To help clarify this, add a placeholder after 1.304 so that it is 1.3040. Compare the numbers in words: one and three thousand forty ten-thousandths is larger than one and three thousand twenty-five ten-thousandths. 1.3040 > 1.3025

EXERCISE
3·9

Circle the correct symbol to make each statement true. Match the letter under the symbol with the number of the problem at the end of the exercise to complete the sentence.

1.   0.75 _____ 0.81

    < > =

    I T N

2.   1.3 _____ 1.4

    < > =

    N Y W

3.   0.120 _____ 0.12

    < > =

    J S A

4.   0.562 _____ 0.561

    < > =

    S T I

5.   2.006 _____ 2.0067

    < > =

    H R M

6. 4.839 _____ 3.839

< > =

L G P

7. 0.0182 _____ 0.02

< > =

M D B

8. 3.095 _____ 3.0950

< > =

H S D

___ ___ ___ ___ ___ ___ ___
 7   3   5   3   4   7   3

___ ___ ___ ___ ___ ___ is known for organizing the civil
 6   3   2   8   5   1

disobedience movement that led to India's independence from Great Britain.

_____

Use >, <, or = to compare each pair of decimals.

1. 0.5 _____ 0.2

2. 0.33 _____ 0.7

3. 1.76 _____ 1.9

4. 1.293 _____ 1.304

5. 0.620 _____ 0.62

6. 2.22 _____ 2.8

7. 1.33 _____ 1.45

8. 5.02 _____ 5.2

9. 2.01 _____ 2.001

10. 0.275 _____ 0.112

11. 0.872 _____ 0.826

12. 8.81 _____ 8.91

13. 1.45 _____ 1.543

14. 0.445 _____ 0.441

15. 2.087 _____ 2.091

16. 5.1205 _____ 5.1250

Ordering decimals

Once you understand how to compare decimals, you can write decimals in order from least to greatest or greatest to least. When comparing several decimals at a time, you may make a table to help you examine the numbers in each place.

Example 1: Write 0.5, 1.25, 0.83, and 0.84 in order from least to greatest.

◆ Make a table with the decimal point in the same place for each number as shown below. Write the digits in their correct place. Fill in the empty places with a zero.

Ones	Decimal Point	Tenths	Hundredths
0	.	5	0
1	.	2	5
0	.	8	3
0	.	8	4

◆ Begin at the left and compare the digits in each place. There is only one 1. The other digits in the ones place are zero. 1.25 is the largest number.

◆ Move to the tenths place and compare the digits. 5, 8, and 8 are in the tenths. (Do not consider the 2 because 1.25 is the largest number.) 8 is the highest number in the tenths place, but there are two 8s. Because there are two 8s in the tenths place, move to the hundredths place. 3 and 4 are in the hundredths place. (Do not consider the 5 because 1.25 is the largest number.) 4 is larger than 3. 0.84 is larger than 0.83.

◆ The last number in the table is 0.5. This is the smallest number in the set.

◆ Write all the numbers in order from least to greatest: 0.5, 0.83, 0.84, 1.25.

Example 2: Write 1.87, 0.991, 0.62, and 1.08 in order from greatest to least.

◆ Instead of using a table to compare the decimals, simply compare the digits by place value.

◆ Begin with the ones place. Two numbers have 1 whole, 1.87 and 1.08. Because 1.87 has 8 tenths, it is larger than 1.08, which has 0 tenths. 1.87 is the largest number. 1.08 is second largest.

◆ Compare the remaining numbers according to the tenths place. 0.991 has 9 tenths, but 0.62 has only 6 tenths. 0.991 is larger than 0.62.

◆ From greatest to least the numbers are 1.87, 1.08, 0.991, and 0.62.

EXERCISE
3·11

Place each set of decimals (with their corresponding letters) in order according to the directions. Write the letter of the fourth number in each set above the number of the problem at the end of the exercise to complete the sentence.

Place the numbers in each set below in order from least to greatest.

1. 1.57, 1.4, 1.9, 1.85, 0.99
   M   H   P   I   W

Place the numbers in each set below in order from greatest to least.

2. 0.75, 0.81, 0.9, 0.45, 0.2
   W   L   E   R   C

3. 0.73, 0.15, 0.22, 0.19, 1.01
   A   T   J   L   C

4. 5.9, 5.32, 4.91, 4.7, 5.5
   U   F   C   M   N

5. 2.05, 2.01, 1.95, 2.4, 2.04
   T   E   Y   B   W

6. 8.25, 8.11, 8.59, 8.257, 8.3
   W   B   Y   O   M

7. 0.34, 0.3, 0.44, 0.6, 0.51
   I   G   D   R   E

8. 0.88, 0.26, 0.78, 0.808, 0.781
   A   F   N   I   S

9. 1.72, 2.1, 1.63, 1.08, 1.9
   R   I   N   O   H

10. 1.24, 1.024, 1.04, 1.4, 1.044
   H   S   G   L   O

11. 3.01, 3.02, 3.002, 3.001, 3.1
   T   L   Y   C   K

The ____ ____ ____ ____ ____   ____ ____ ____ ____ of
   10   2   7   3   5   6   3   11   11

____ ____ ____ ____ ____ is the only man-made structure on Earth
 4   9   1   8   3

that can be seen from the moon. It was built over a 2,000-year period and measures 5,500 miles long.

EXERCISE
3·12

Place the following decimals in order from least to greatest.

1. 0.5, 0.4, 0.7, 0.9, 1

2. 0.42, 0.71, 0.88, 0.4, 0.7

3. 1.3, 1.67, 1.9, 1.32, 1.55

4. 2.003, 2.04, 2.005, 2.1, 2.02

5. 4.3, 3.4, 5.1, 2.7, 1.08

6. 0.905, 0.805, 0.923, 0.799, 0.089

7. 3.75, 3.79, 2.58, 2.33, 4.01

8. 1.55, 1.072, 1.505, 1.63, 1.064

Place the following decimals in order from greatest to least.

9. 7.304, 7.062, 7.51, 7.3, 7.4

10. 0.354, 0.382, 0.592, 0.491, 0.399

11. 5.011, 5.002, 5.0385, 5.0183, 5

12. 10.7, 10.28, 10.9, 1.08, 1.02

13. 1.048, 1.4, 1.028, 1.94, 1.09

14. 0.002, 0.202, 0.0002, 0.02, 0.2

15. 3.928, 3.174, 3.172, 3.1, 3.22

16. 8.293, 8.8, 8.01, 8.29, 8.23

Operations with decimals

·4·

Estimating sums and differences

When adding or subtracting decimals, estimating answers can help you decide if your actual answer is reasonable. Before you can estimate a sum or difference, you must round the numbers. Follow these rules to round numbers:

1. Find the place you must round to. Underline the digit in this place.

2. Look at the digit to the right of the place you must round.

   ◆ If it is less than 5, the underlined digit stays the same. This is called "rounding down."

   ◆ If it is 5 or more, add 1 to the underlined digit. This is called "rounding up."

3. Change all digits to the right of the rounded digit to zeros.

4. Delete any zeros that are not placeholders. (There must always be a digit in the place you are rounding to, even if the digit is zero.)

Example: Round 1.682 *to the nearest tenth.*

   ◆ Underline the digit in the tenths place in 1.682. 6 is in the tenths place. 1.<u>6</u>82

   ◆ Look at the digit to the right of 6, which is 8. 8 is greater than 6, which means you must round up. Add 1 to 6 to find 7. Place 7 in the tenths place. Change the other digits to the right of the tenths place to zeros. 1.700

   ◆ Omit the zeros in 1.700. They are unnecessary because you are rounding to the tenths place.

   ◆ 1.682 rounded to the tenths place is 1.7.

Sometimes, a 9 will be in the place you are rounding to. When this happens, follow these steps:

1. Find the place you must round to. Underline the digit in this place, which would be 9.

2. If the digit to the right of the 9 is less than 5, the 9 stays the same. If the digit to the right of the 9 is 5 or more, you must round the 9 up by adding 1 to it.

3. When you add 1 to 9, the sum is 10. Write a 0 in place of the 9 and add 1 to the digit to the left.

4. Change all digits to the right of the rounded number to zeros.

5. Delete any zeros that are not placeholders. (There must always be a digit in the place you are rounding to, even if the digit is zero.)

Example: Round 1.796 to the nearest hundredth.

◆ Underline the digit in the hundredths place in 1.796. 1.7<u>9</u>6

◆ Look at the digit to the right of 9. Because it is 6, round up. Write 0 in place of the 9 and add 1 to 7, which is 8. Change all the digits to the right of the hundredths place to zeros. 1.800

◆ Because you are rounding to the nearest hundredth, there must be a digit in the hundredths place. Omit the zero in the thousandths place. 1.796 rounded to the nearest hundredth is 1.80.

To estimate sums and differences of decimals, round each decimal to the nearest whole number. Then add or subtract. Use the ≈ symbol, which means "is approximately equal to," to show that the sum or difference is an estimate.

Example 1: Estimate the sum. 1.5 + 2.3

◆ Round 1.5 and 2.3 to the nearest whole numbers, which are in the ones place. Follow the steps above for rounding.

◆ 1.5 is rounded to 2. 2.3 is rounded to 2.

◆ Add. $2 + 2 = 4$

◆ $1.5 + 2.3 \approx 4$

Example 2: Estimate the difference. 5.7 − 3.27

◆ Round 5.7 and 3.27 to the nearest whole numbers.

◆ 5.7 is rounded to 6 and 3.27 is rounded to 3.

◆ Subtract. $6 − 3 = 3$

◆ $5.7 − 3.27 \approx 3$

Round to the nearest tenth.

1. 0.83

2. 1.57

Round to the nearest hundredth.

3. 1.572

4. 4.098

Round to the nearest whole number.

5. 0.894

6. 3.729

Round to the nearest thousandth.

7. 1.3829

8. 0.9289

Estimate each sum or difference by rounding to the nearest whole number.

9. 1.42 + 1.59

10. 2.09 + 3.84

11. 5.92 − 4.87

12. 0.5 − 0.99

13. $8.95 + 4.2$

14. $4.283 - 2.8472$

15. $5.3 - 0.999$

16. $7.8294 + 5.3285$

Addition and subtraction of decimals

Adding and subtracting decimals is similar to adding and subtracting whole numbers. But you must align the numbers according to place value. Follow these steps to add or subtract decimals:

1. Line up the numbers vertically according to their place value. Line up the decimal points and keep the columns straight.

2. Add zeros as placeholders, if necessary.

3. Bring the decimal point straight down.

4. Add or subtract as you would add or subtract whole numbers.

Example 1: $1.357 + 0.58$

◆ Rewrite the problem vertically and line up the decimal points. Add a zero after the 8 in 0.58 because 1.357 has a digit in the thousandths place and 0.58 does not. The zero holds the thousandths place.

$$\begin{array}{r} 1.357 \\ + 0.580 \\ \hline \end{array}$$

◆ Bring the decimal point straight down.

◆ Add as you would add whole numbers.

$$\begin{array}{r} 0.580 \\ + 1.357 \\ \hline 1.937 \end{array}$$

Example 2: $3.2 - 1.56$

◆ Rewrite the problem vertically and line up the decimal points. Add a zero in the hundredths place in 3.2 to hold the place.

```
  3.20
- 1.56
```

◆ Bring the decimal point straight down.

◆ Subtract as you would subtract whole numbers.

```
  3.20
- 1.56
  1.64
```

EXERCISE
4·2

Add or subtract. Write the letter of the problem in the space above its answer at the end of the exercise to complete the sentence. Some answers will be used twice.

N.   0.54 + 0.28

O.   1.38 + 2.75

L.   3.5 − 2.1

A.   0.99 − 0.4

K.   4.7 + 3.02

E.   3.12 − 1.1

T.   5.1 + 2

S.   0.82 − 0.2

F.   8.92 − 5.74

R. 4 + 4.35

V. 10.5 – 6.83

I. 2.05 + 2.77

___ ___ ___ ___ ___ ___ ___ ___ D.
3.18 8.35 0.59 0.82 7.72 1.4 4.82 0.82

___ ___ ___ ___ ___ ___ ___ ___ ___ is the only US
8.35 4.13 4.13 0.62 2.02 3.67 2.02 1.4 7.1

president to serve more than two terms in office. In fact, he was elected to four terms!

EXERCISE
4·3

Add or subtract.

1. 0.5 + 0.3

2. 0.9 + 0.77

3. 0.45 – 0.21

4. 1.4 – 1.2

5. 1.7 + 2.8

6. 2 + 3.73

7. 0.52 – 0.395

8. $3.21 + 4.204$

9. $0.427 + 4.2$

10. $5.028 - 3.03$

11. $5.502 + 3.8$

12. $0.824 - 0.6$

13. $1.938 - 0.58$

14. $4.8203 - 3.014$

15. $9.492 + 3.501$

16. $8.2043 - 3.59$

Multiplication of decimals

Multiplying decimals is similar to multiplying whole numbers, except that you must account for the decimal point in your product. Follow these steps:

1. Line up the number by columns. Do not line up the decimal points. Place the number with the larger number of digits on top.

2. Multiply as you would multiply whole numbers.

3. Decide where to write the decimal point in your answer. Count the number of places held by the digits to the right of the decimal point in the first factor. Then, count the number of places held by the digits to the right of the decimal point in the second factor. Find the sum of the number of places.

4. Start at the right of your product and count the same number of places to the left. Write the decimal point there. If there are not enough numbers in the product to correctly place the decimal point, add zeros as placeholders, and then write the decimal point.

Example 1: 0.5 × 0.572

♦ Line up the numbers by columns. Because 0.572 has more digits than 0.5, place it on top. Remember that lining up the decimal point is unnecessary for multiplication.

    0.572
  × 0.5

♦ Multiply as you would multiply whole numbers.

    0.572
  × 0.5
    2860

♦ Decide where to write the decimal point. There are three digits to the right of the decimal point in 0.572 and one digit to the right of the decimal point in 0.5. Because there is a total of four digits to the right of the decimal points in the factors, there must be four digits to the right of the decimal point in the product.

♦ Start at the right of 2860, count four places to the left, and write the decimal point. The product is 0.2860. Because the zero in the ten-thousandths place can be omitted, the product is 0.286.

Example 2: 0.32 × 0.823

♦ Line up the numbers.

    0.823
  × 0.32

♦ Multiply as you would multiply whole numbers.

    0.823
  × 0.32
    1646
   24690
   26336

♦ A total of five digits are to the right of the decimal points in the factors. The product must have five digits to the right of the decimal point.

♦ Start at the right of 26336 and count five places to the left. Write a decimal point in front of the 2. The product is 0.26336.

Example 3: 0.0048 × 7

♦ Line up the numbers. (Notice that 7 is a whole number. Written as a decimal, the whole number 7 is 7.0, but the decimal point and zero are unnecessary and are omitted.)

```
  0.0048
x      7
```

- Multiply as you would multiply whole numbers.

```
  0.0048
x      7
   336
```

- Because a total of four digits are to the right of the decimal point in the factors, there must be four digits to the right of the decimal point in the product.

- Start at the right of 336 and count four places to the left. Notice there are only three places in 336. You must write a zero in front of the first 3 as a placeholder. Then write the decimal point. The product is 0.0336.

EXERCISE 4·4

Multiply. Write the letter of the problem in the space above its answer at the end of the exercise to complete the sentence. Some answers will be used twice.

E. 1.5 × 0.8

L. 0.9 × 0.56

O. 2.5 × 0.85

B. 3.8 × 1.7

R. 4 × 0.6

T. 0.04 × 0.3

A. 0.35 × 0.2

S. 3 × 0.9

| 2.4 | 2.125 | 6.46 | 1.2 | 2.4 | 0.012 | | 0.504 | 0.07 |

_____ _____ _____ _____ _____ was the first European to sail down the
2.7 0.07 0.504 0.504 1.2

Mississippi River from the Great Lakes to the Gulf of Mexico. He began this journey on February 13, 1682, and reached the Gulf of Mexico on April 9 of the same year.

EXERCISE 4·5

Multiply.

1. 0.7×0.6

2. 0.58×0.23

3. 0.4×0.95

4. 1.9×0.85

5. 3.5×0.6

6. 1.3×3.21

7. 4.8×0.682

8. 5×0.3

9. 0.6×7

10. 9.23×0.03

11. 0.91×0.734

12. 0.02×0.05

13. 7.02×0.8

14. 4.204×3.5

15. 0.582×2

16. 6.01×3.055

Division of decimals by whole numbers

Dividing a decimal by a whole number is similar to dividing whole numbers. The only difference is that a decimal point must be placed in the answer. Follow these steps to divide decimals by whole numbers:

1. Place the decimal point in the quotient (the answer to a division problem) directly above the decimal point in the dividend (the number that is being divided).

2. Divide as you would divide whole numbers. (Use zeros as placeholders, if necessary.)

3. If a number or group of numbers repeats in the quotient and does not terminate, place a repetend over the number or numbers that repeat.

Example 1: $0.45 \div 5$

◆ Rewrite the problem.

$$5\overline{)0.45}$$

◆ Place the decimal point in the quotient directly above the decimal point in the dividend, and divide as you would divide whole numbers. Write a zero as a placeholder in the ones place and in the tenths place in the quotient. The quotient is 0.09.

$$
\begin{array}{r}
0.09 \\
5\overline{)0.45} \\
\underline{45} \\
0
\end{array}
$$

Example 2: 1.28 ÷ 4

◆ Rewrite the problem.

$$4\overline{)1.28}$$

◆ Place the decimal point in the quotient directly above the decimal point in the dividend, and divide as you would divide whole numbers. Write a zero as a placeholder in the ones place. The quotient is 0.32.

```
      0.32
 4 ) 1.28
     12
      8
      8
      0
```

Example 3: 6.25 ÷ 3

◆ Rewrite the problem.

$$3\overline{)6.25}$$

◆ Place the decimal point in the quotient directly above the decimal point in the dividend, and divide as you would divide whole numbers. Notice that you must add zeros to keep dividing. The remainder continues to be 1, and 3 repeats in the quotient. You must put a repetend over the 3 to show that it repeats. The quotient is a repeating decimal, $2.08\overline{3}$.

```
       2.0833 = 2.08̄3
 3 ) 6.2500
     6
     0.2
       0
       25
       24
        10
         9
        10
         9
         1
```

Divide. Write the letter of the problem in the space above its answer at the end of the exercise to complete the sentence. Some answers will be used twice.

A. $1.5 \div 3$

M. $3.2 \div 4$

D. $2.25 \div 5$

R. $3.64 \div 3$

O. $7.82 \div 4$

S. $81.9 \div 9$

G. $34.8 \div 8$

N. $52.6 \div 8$

Most of the planets in our solar system are named for

____ ____ ____ ____ ____   ____ ____ ____ ____.
1.21$\overline{3}$ 1.955 0.8   0.5   6.575   4.35 1.955 0.45   9.1

Divide.

1. $6.3 \div 3$

2. $2.4 \div 6$

3. $5.6 \div 8$

4. $2.1 \div 7$

5. $10.5 \div 5$

6. $3.69 \div 6$

7. $27.5 \div 10$

8. $4.58 \div 8$

9. $8.62 \div 4$

10. $6.71 \div 3$

11. $9.86 \div 6$

12. $82.5 \div 5$

13. $30.3 \div 3$

14. $67.8 \div 8$

15. $9.14 \div 9$

16. $8.42 \div 3$

Division of decimals by decimals

When dividing a decimal by a decimal, you must change the divisor to a whole number. You do this by multiplying the divisor by 10, 100, or 1,000, depending on the number of decimal places in the divisor. Whatever number you multiply the divisor by, you must also multiply the dividend by. Follow these steps:

1. Move the decimal point to the right of the divisor, expressing the divisor as a whole number. Moving the decimal point is the same as multiplying by a power of 10.

2. Move the decimal point in the dividend to the right the same number of places. This is the same as multiplying by a power of 10. If there are not enough places, add a zero or zeros to the right of the number. Write the decimal point after the correct number of places.

3. Place the decimal point in the quotient directly above the decimal point in the dividend.

4. Divide as you would divide whole numbers.

5. If a remainder repeats, add zeros to continue dividing. Write a repetend over the number or group of numbers in the quotient that repeats.

Example 1: $4.55 \div 0.5$

- Rewrite the problem.

$$0.5 \overline{)4.55}$$

- Move the decimal point one place to the right in the divisor so that the divisor is a whole number. Then move the decimal point one place to the right in the dividend. In both cases, this is the same as multiplying by 10.

$$5 \overline{)45.5} \quad \frac{9.1}{}$$

- Write the decimal point in the quotient directly above the decimal point in the dividend, and divide as you would divide whole numbers. The quotient is 9.1.

$$
\begin{array}{r}
9.1 \\
5 \overline{)45.5} \\
\underline{45} \\
5 \\
\underline{5} \\
0
\end{array}
$$

Example 2: $3.6 \div 0.16$

- Rewrite the problem.

$$0.16 \overline{)3.6}$$

- Move the decimal point two places to the right in the divisor so that the divisor is a whole number. Then move the decimal point two places to the right in the dividend. In both cases, this is the same as multiplying by 100. You must add a zero in the dividend.

$$16\overline{)360}$$

- Divide as you would divide whole numbers. Because there is a remainder, add a decimal point and a zero and continue dividing until there is no remainder. Remember to write the decimal point in the quotient directly above the decimal point in the dividend. The quotient is 22.5.

```
      22.5
16)360.0
    32
    40
    32
     80
     80
      0
```

Example 3: $6.63 \div 0.9$

- Rewrite the problem.

$$0.9\overline{)6.63}$$

- Move the decimal point in the divisor one place to right. Then move the decimal point in the dividend one place to the right. In both cases, this is the same as multiplying by 10.

$$9\overline{)66.3}$$

- Write the decimal point in the quotient directly above the decimal point in the dividend, and divide as you would divide whole numbers. Notice that a remainder repeats. The quotient is a repeating decimal, $7.3\overline{6}$.

```
      7.366 = 7.36̄
9)66.300
    63
    33
    27
     60
     54
      60
      54
       6
```

Divide. Write the letter of the problem in the space above its answer at the end of the exercise to complete the sentence. Some answers will be used twice. Some answers will not be used.

S. $6.52 \div 0.4$

N. $2.45 \div 0.5$

U. $4.14 \div 0.8$

T. $46.6 \div 3.3$

P. $72.2 \div 3.6$

V. $8.2 \div 0.4$

E. $9.87 \div 0.72$

O. $38.4 \div 0.6$

M. $12.4 \div 0.25$

I. $6.2 \div 1.2$

In Italy, in AD 79, ____ ____ ____ ____ ____
                      49.6   64   5.175   4.9   14.$\overline{12}$

____ ____ ____ ____ ____ ____ ____ ____
20.5 13.708$\overline{3}$ 16.3   5.175   20.5   5.1$\overline{6}$ 5.175   16.3

erupted and buried the city of Pompeii in volcanic ash.

Divide.

1. $9.6 \div 0.3$

2. $6.24 \div 0.4$

3. $8.13 \div 0.3$

4. $5.25 \div 1.5$

5. $18.6 \div 0.6$

6. $4.97 \div 0.7$

7. $34.8 \div 1.8$

8. $2.01 \div 0.4$

9. $7.24 \div 2.4$

10. $5.23 \div 0.9$

11. $7.32 \div 2.4$

12. $9.61 \div 3.3$

13. $17.2 \div 2.2$

14. $0.4 \div 0.25$

15. $0.82 \div 0.04$

16. $9.41 \div 0.3$

EXERCISE 4·10

Perform the indicated operation.

1. $4.5 + 2.75$

2. 0.57×1.4

3. $5.88 - 2.7$

4. $15 \div 0.3$

5. $14.2 \div 1.2$

6. $9.203 - 0.57$

7. $33.2 \div 4$

8. 4.02×0.82

9. $8 \div 0.45$

10. $7.94 - 1.384$

11. $6.07 + 0.297$

12. 0.24×0.99

13. 0.98 − 0.576

14. 3.12 ÷ 2.4

15. 5.04 × 0.7

16. 6.7 ÷ 8

Connecting fractions, decimals, and percents

The meaning of percent

A percent is a ratio of a number to 100. *Percent* means "per hundred." The symbol for a percent is %.

Percents are easy to visualize using a 10-by-10 grid because there are 100 small squares in the grid. In the figure that follows, you can find the percent of the grid that is shaded by counting the number of shaded squares. 50 squares, half of the grid, are shaded. Because a percent compares a number to 100, the percent of squares that are shaded is 50%, or 50 out of 100.

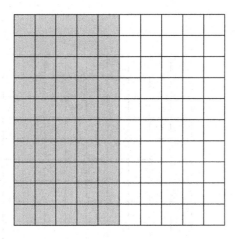

Example: Write a percent to describe the shaded part of the grid.

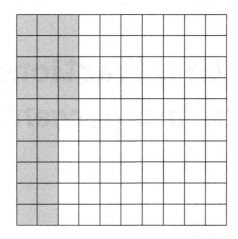

Count the number of shaded squares. 25 squares are shaded. This represents 25%.

Write a percent to describe the part of the grid that is shaded.

1.

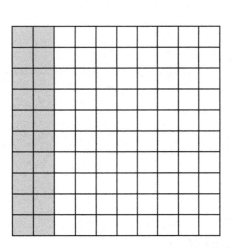

2.

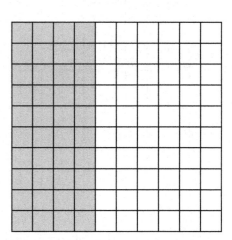

3.

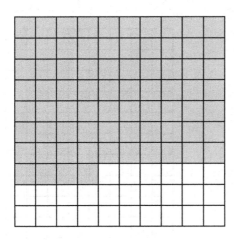

4.

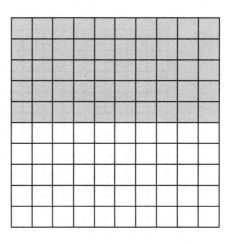

5.

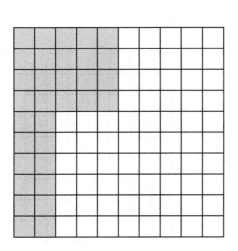

6.

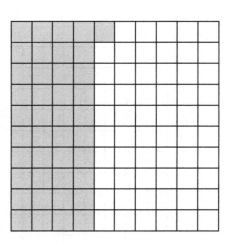

Shade the indicated amount.

7.   80%

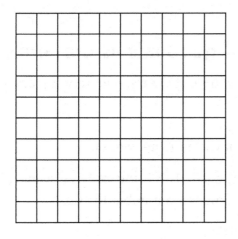

8.   30%

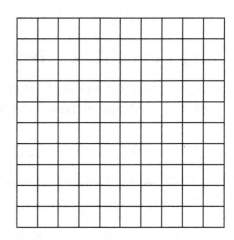

9. 71%

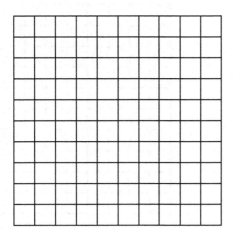

10. 58%

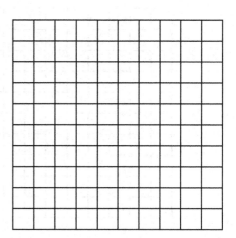

11. 12%

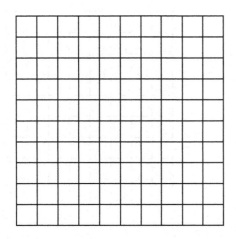

12. 95%

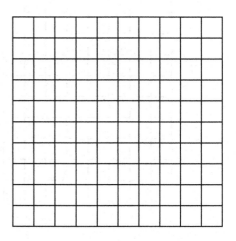

Writing percents as decimals and decimals as percents

Because a percent is a ratio of a number to 100, you must use the hundredths place when writing percents as decimals. Follow these steps:

1. Write the number of the percent. Do not write the percent sign.

2. Move the decimal point two places to the left. This is the same as dividing by 100. You must divide by 100 because a percent compares a number to 100.

3. Eliminate any zeros that are not placeholders.

Example 1: Write 40% as a decimal.

- Write 40.

- Move the decimal point two places to the left. 40% = 0.40 or 0.4

- You may also use your knowledge of place value to write 40% as a decimal. Since percents are a ratio of a number to 100, 40% represents 40 hundredths, or 0.40.

Example 2: Write 5% as a decimal.

- Write 5.

- Move the decimal point two places to the left. Because there are not enough digits in 5 to move the decimal point two places to the left, add a zero in front of the 5 as a placeholder. 5% = 0.05.

- You may also use place value. 5% represents 5 hundredths, which is written as 0.05.

Use the following steps to write a decimal as a percent. Note that decimals larger than 1 equal percents larger than 100%.

1. Write the decimal. Then move the decimal point two places to the right. This is the same as multiplying by 100. Add zeros as placeholders, if necessary.

2. Write the percent sign.

Example 1: Write 0.42 as a percent.

- Write 0.42. Then move the decimal point two places to the right. Write the percent sign. 0.42 = 42%.

- You may also use place value. 0.42 represents 42 hundredths, which equals 42%.

Example 2: Write 0.9 as a percent.

- Write 0.9. Then move the decimal point two places to the right. Because there are not enough digits in 0.9, add a zero after the 9 to hold a place. 0.90 Write the percent sign. 0.9 = 0.90 = 90%

- You may also use place value. 0.9 = 0.90, which represents 90 hundredths, or 90%.

Find the equivalent decimal for each percent. Write the letter of the problem in the space above its answer at the end of the exercise to complete the sentence. Some answers will be used twice. One answer will not be used.

D. 80%

V. 36%

I. 8%

Y. 100%

H. 1.5%

L. 6.7%

Find the equivalent percent for each decimal. Write the letter of the problem in the space above its answer at the end of the exercise to complete the sentence. Some answers will be used twice. Some answers will not be used.

N. 0.15

O. 0.94

W. 1.5

E. 0.036

C. 0.09

T. 0.67

An anemometer is a device that measures ____ ____ ____ ____
                                        150% 0.08 15% 0.8

____ ____ ____ ____ ____ ____ ____ ____.
0.36 3.6% 0.067 94% 9% 0.08 67% 1

It was invented by an Italian architect named Leon Battista Alberti in 1450.

5·3

Write each percent as an equivalent decimal.

1. 45%

2. 75%

3. 12%

4. 5.8%

5. 88%

6. 91.2%

7. 13.5%

8. 120%

Write each decimal as an equivalent percent.

9. 0.38

10. 0.14

11. 0.79

12. 0.472

13. 0.082

14. 0.03

15. 1.35

16. 1.9

Writing fractions and mixed numbers as percents

There are two methods for changing fractions and mixed numbers to percents.

Method 1: Change the fraction to a percent using an equivalent fraction

A percent represents the ratio of a number to 100. A fraction can also represent the ratio of a number to 100. When converting a fraction to a percent, the denominator of the fraction must be 100. To use this method, write an equivalent fraction whose denominator is 100. The numerator represents the percent. Note that this method is practical only when the denominator of the fraction is a factor of 100.

Example 1: Change $\frac{4}{5}$ to a percent.

- The denominator, 5, is a factor of 100. Write an equivalent fraction with a denominator of 100. $\frac{4}{5} = \frac{4 \times 20}{5 \times 20} = \frac{80}{100}$
- The numerator, 80, represents the percent. $\frac{4}{5} = \frac{80}{100} = 80\%$

Example 2: Change $2\frac{1}{2}$ to a percent.

- Work with the fraction first. The denominator, 2, is a factor of 100. Write an equivalent fraction with a denominator of 100. $\frac{1}{2} = \frac{1 \times 50}{2 \times 50} = \frac{50}{100} = 50\%$
- But you also have 2 wholes. Since each whole represents 100%, 2 wholes equal 200%. $2\frac{1}{2} = 200\% + 50\% = 250\%$

Method 2: Change the fraction to a decimal and then to a percent

This method must be used when the fraction is not equivalent to a fraction with a denominator of 100. First, change the fraction to a decimal by dividing the numerator by the denominator. Then change the decimal to a percent by moving the decimal point two places to the right and writing the percent sign. This method will work with all fractions.

Example 1: Change $\frac{1}{8}$ to a percent.

♦ Change the fraction to a decimal by dividing the numerator by the denominator. Remember to add zeros to continue dividing if there is a remainder.

$$
\begin{array}{r}
0.125 \\
8\overline{)1.000} \\
\underline{8} \\
20 \\
\underline{16} \\
40 \\
\underline{40} \\
0
\end{array}
$$

♦ Move the decimal point two places to the right and write the percent sign.
$$\frac{1}{8} = 0.125 = 12.5\%$$

Example 2: Change $4\frac{4}{6}$ to a percent.

♦ Work with the fraction first. Change $\frac{5}{6}$ to a decimal by dividing the numerator by the denominator. A remainder of 2 continues, which means that the decimal does not terminate. 3 repeats in the quotient.

$$
\begin{array}{r}
0.833 = 0.8\overline{3} \\
6\overline{)5.000} \\
\underline{48} \\
20 \\
\underline{18} \\
20 \\
\underline{18} \\
2
\end{array}
$$

♦ Express $0.8\overline{3}$ as a percent by moving the decimal point two places to the left and writing the percent sign. $0.8\overline{3} = 83.\overline{3}\%$ Add 4 wholes, which are 400%.
$4\frac{5}{6} = 400\% + 83.\overline{3}\% = 483.\overline{3}\%$. Remember to keep the repetend, the line above the digit or digits that repeats, when you convert repeating decimals to a percent.

Find the equivalent percent for each fraction. Write the letter of the problem in the space above its answer at the end of the exercise to complete the sentence. Some answers will be used twice. One answer will not be used.

A. $\dfrac{3}{5}$

L. $\dfrac{5}{8}$

D. $\dfrac{3}{10}$

M. $\dfrac{18}{20}$

H. $1\dfrac{7}{10}$

I. $\dfrac{1}{3}$

Y. $\dfrac{4}{11}$

S. $1\dfrac{3}{8}$

T. $1\dfrac{12}{18}$

N. $1\dfrac{21}{22}$

_____ _____ _____ _____ _____ _____ _____ _____ was known as

166.$\overline{6}$%   170%   60%   33.$\overline{3}$%   62.5%   60%   195.$\overline{45}$%   30%

_____ _____ _____ _____ until the late 1940s. Its name now means

137.5%   33.$\overline{3}$%   60%   90%

"land of the free."

Write each fraction or mixed number as a percent.

1. $\dfrac{7}{10}$

2. $\dfrac{1}{5}$

3. $\dfrac{2}{9}$

4. $\dfrac{7}{8}$

5. $2\dfrac{1}{4}$

6. $1\dfrac{2}{3}$

7. $1\dfrac{3}{4}$

8. $\dfrac{11}{12}$

9. $2\dfrac{7}{15}$

10. $\dfrac{8}{20}$

11. $\dfrac{1}{6}$

12. $3\dfrac{3}{10}$

13. $\dfrac{4}{25}$

14. $1\dfrac{1}{50}$

15. $\frac{13}{15}$

16. $3\frac{5}{9}$

Writing percents as fractions or mixed numbers

Any percent can be written as a fraction or mixed number in lowest terms. Because a percent represents the ratio of a number to 100, a percent can be expressed as an equivalent fraction with a denominator of 100.

Example 1: Change 70% to a fraction.

♦ Write 70% as a fraction. $\frac{70}{100}$

♦ Simplify $\frac{70}{100}$ by dividing the numerator and denominator by 10. $\frac{70}{100} = \frac{70 \div 10}{100 \div 10} = \frac{7}{10}$

♦ 70% = $\frac{7}{10}$.

Example 2: Change 150% to a mixed number.

♦ Write 150% as an improper fraction. $\frac{150}{100}$

♦ Simplify $\frac{150}{100}$ by dividing the numerator and denominator by 50. $\frac{150}{100} = \frac{150 \div 50}{100 \div 50} = \frac{3}{2}$

♦ Since the numerator is larger than the denominator, change the fraction to a mixed number. $\frac{3}{2} = 1\frac{1}{2}$

♦ 150% = $1\frac{1}{2}$

When the percent is a mixed number (or can be expressed as a mixed number), change the number to an improper fraction. Then multiply by $\frac{1}{100}$.

Example 1: Change $12\frac{1}{2}$% to a fraction.

♦ Change $12\frac{1}{2}$ to an improper fraction. $12\frac{1}{2} = \frac{25}{2}$

♦ Multiply by $\frac{1}{100}$. Use the shortcut or simplify after you multiply. $\frac{\overset{1}{\cancel{25}}}{2} \times \frac{1}{\underset{4}{\cancel{100}}} = \frac{1}{8}$ (This example shows the shortcut.)

♦ $12\frac{1}{2}\% = \frac{1}{8}$

Example 2: Change $133\frac{1}{3}$% to a fraction.

- Change $133\frac{1}{3}$ to an improper fraction. $133\frac{1}{3} = \frac{400}{3}$

- Multiply by $\frac{1}{100}$. Use the shortcut or simplify after you multiply. $\frac{400}{3} \times \frac{1}{100} = \frac{400}{300} = \frac{4}{3} = 1\frac{1}{3}$
(This example shows the multiplication and simplified answer.)

- $133\frac{1}{3}\% = 1\frac{1}{3}$

Example 3: Change 15.8% to a fraction.

- Change 15.8 to a mixed number. $15.8 = 15\frac{8}{10}$, which can be simplified to $15\frac{4}{5}$.

- Change $15\frac{4}{5}$ to an improper fraction. $15\frac{4}{5} = \frac{75}{5}$

- Multiply by $\frac{1}{100}$. $\frac{79}{5} \times \frac{1}{100} = \frac{79}{500}$, which is in simplest form.

- $15.8\% = \frac{79}{500}$

EXERCISE

5·6

Find the equivalent fraction or mixed number for each percent. Write the letter of the problem in the space above its answer at the end of the exercise to complete the sentence. Some answers will be used twice. Some answers will not be used.

O. 17%

M. 52%

P. 40.5%

S. 120%

A. 36%

E. $8\frac{1}{3}\%$

R. 135%

H. 75%

N. $83\frac{1}{3}\%$

I. 195%

The Middle Ages began with the collapse of the

$\underline{}$ $\underline{}$ $\underline{}$ $\underline{}$ $\underline{}$ $\quad$ $\underline{}$ $\underline{}$ $\underline{}$ $\underline{}$ $\underline{}$ $\underline{}$.

$1\frac{7}{20}$ $\quad$ $\frac{17}{100}$ $\quad$ $\frac{13}{25}$ $\quad$ $\frac{9}{25}$ $\quad$ $\frac{5}{6}$ $\qquad$ $\frac{1}{12}$ $\quad$ $\frac{13}{25}$ $\quad$ $\frac{81}{200}$ $\quad$ $1\frac{19}{20}$ $\quad$ $1\frac{7}{20}$ $\quad$ $\frac{1}{12}$

This was a time of great turmoil in Europe.

EXERCISE
5·7

Write each percent as a fraction or mixed number.

1. 10%

2. 25%

3. 45%

4. 95.2%

5. 3%

6. 175%

7. 48.5%

8. 130%

9. $66\frac{2}{3}\%$

10. 5%

11. $111\frac{1}{9}\%$

12. 63%

13. 190%

14. 248.9%

15. 83%

16. 305.2%

Complete the chart by filling in the missing equivalent values for each row.

	Fraction or mixed number	Decimal	Percent
1.	$\frac{1}{4}$		
2.		0.75	
3.			100%
4.		1.3	
5.	$\frac{5}{6}$		
6.			78%
7.	$\frac{9}{10}$		
8.		0.3	
9.			149%
10.	$\frac{1}{50}$		
11.			1%
12.	$\frac{5}{8}$		
13.		$0.\overline{09}$	
14.			7%
15.	$\frac{1}{12}$		
16.			$266.\overline{6}\%$

Operations with percents

Finding the percent of a number

You can find the percent of a number by changing the percent to a decimal and multiplying. Remember that the word *of* in mathematics indicates multiplication. When you are finding the percent *of* a number, multiply.

Example 1: What is 40% of 90?

- Change 40% to a decimal. 40% = 0.40 or 0.4 You can eliminate zeros that are not placeholders.

- Multiply 0.4 by 90.

$$
\begin{array}{r}
90 \\
\times\, 0.4 \\
\hline
36.0
\end{array}
$$

- 40% of 90 is 36.

Example 2: What is 95% of 250?

- Change 95% to a decimal. 95% = 0.95

- Multiply 0.95 by 250.

$$
\begin{array}{r}
250 \\
\times\, 0.95 \\
\hline
1250 \\
22500 \\
\hline
237.50
\end{array}
$$

  You can eliminate the zero.

- 95% of 250 is 237.5.

Example 3: What is $66\frac{2}{3}$% of 18?

- Change $66\frac{2}{3}$% to a fraction. $66\frac{2}{3}\% = \frac{200}{3} \times \frac{1}{100} = \frac{2}{3}$

- Multiply $\frac{3}{2}$ by 18. $\frac{2}{3} \times \frac{18}{1} = 12$

- $66\frac{2}{3}$% of 18 is 12.

EXERCISE 6·1

Find the percent of each number. Write the letter of the problem in the space above its answer at the end of the exercise to complete the sentence. Some answers will be used more than once. Some answers will not be used.

O. 30% of 30

L. $83\frac{1}{3}\%$ of 60

T. 50% of 80

C. 75% of 200

A. 62% of 135

B. $22\frac{2}{9}\%$ of 72

I. 5% of 15

N. 2% of 50

K. 82% of 70

S. 100% of 20

Frederick Douglass was a famous

—— —— —— —— —— —— —— —— —— —— —— ——
83.7　16　9　50　0.75　40　0.75　9　1　0.75　20　40

who was once a slave. In 1838, he escaped from slavery and gave countless speeches in of favor freedom and even became an advisor to Abraham Lincoln.

Find the percent of each number.

1. 45% of 60

2. 17% of 92

3. 10% of 50

4. 40% of 40

5. 25% of 100

6. 50% of 90

7. 20% of 60

8. 100% of 30

9. 150% of 25

10. 85% of 200

11. 94% of 65

12. 125% of 25

13. $44\frac{4}{9}$% of 36

14. 1% of 200

15. 170% of 95

16. $33\frac{1}{3}$% of 33

Finding what percent one number is of another

To solve problems where you must find what percent one number is of another, you must write and solve a proportion. An example of a proportion is shown here.

$\frac{2}{5} = \frac{x}{10}$

There are two methods for solving a proportion: writing an equivalent fraction and using cross-multiplication.

Method 1: Write an equivalent fraction

Use this method when the larger denominator is a multiple of the smaller denominator.

Example: $\frac{2}{5} = \frac{x}{10}$

◆ In order to find what *x* equals, first find what number times 5 equals 10. 2 × 5 = 10
Because you are multiplying the denominator by 2, you must multiply the numerator by 2. $\frac{2}{5} = \frac{2 \times 2}{5 \times 2} = \frac{4}{10}$

◆ Because $\frac{2}{5} = \frac{4}{10}$, *x* = 4.

Method 2: Use cross-multiplication

Use this method when the larger denominator is not a multiple of the smaller denominator.

Example: $\frac{3}{9} = \frac{x}{15}$

◆ Multiply the first numerator by the second denominator, and multiply the first denominator by the second numerator (in this case, *x*). Notice that the terms you are multiplying are opposites and are diagonally across the equal sign. 3 × 15 = 45 and 9 × *x* = 9*x*

◆ Write the new equation. 45 = 9*x*

◆ Solve this equation by dividing both sides by the coefficient (the number before the variable *x*). $\frac{45}{9} = \frac{9x}{9}$

◆ Because 45 ÷ 9 = 5 and 9*x* ÷ 9 = *x*, *x* = 5.

Proportions are useful in solving different types of percent problems. When you are asked to find what percent one number is of another, you must first set up a proportion.

Example 1: 10 is what percent of 50?

- Decide what number represents the *part* and what number represents the *whole*. 10 is the part and 50 is the whole.

- Write this ratio as a fraction. $\frac{10}{50}$

- Write a proportion relating $\frac{10}{50}$ to a percent. Because a percent represents the ratio of a number to 100, 100 is the denominator. Label the numerator x because the percent is unknown. $\frac{10}{50} = \frac{x}{100}$

- Solve the proportion. Because 100 is a multiple of 50, use Method 1 and write an equivalent fraction. $\frac{10}{50} = \frac{10 \times 2}{50 \times 2} = \frac{20}{100}$

- Because $\frac{10}{50} = \frac{20}{100}$, $x = 20$.

- 10 is 20% of 50.

Example 2: 15 is what percent of 16?

- Decide what number represents the part and what number represents the whole. 15 is the part and 16 is the whole.

- Write this ratio as a fraction. $\frac{15}{16}$

- Write a proportion relating $\frac{15}{16}$ to a percent. $\frac{15}{16} = \frac{x}{100}$

- Solve the proportion. Because 100 is not a multiple of 16, use Method 2 and cross multiply. $15 \times 100 = 16 \times x$

- Write the new equation. $1,500 = 16x$

- To solve for x, divide both sides of the equation by 16.
  $$\frac{1,500}{16} = \frac{16x}{16}$$
  $x = 93.75$

- 15 is 93.75% of 16.

Solve each problem. Write the letter of the problem in the space above its answer at the end of the exercise to complete the sentence. One letter will be used twice.

U. $\dfrac{3}{5} = \dfrac{x}{25}$

N. $\dfrac{1}{8} = \dfrac{x}{12}$

I. $\dfrac{7}{10} = \dfrac{x}{40}$

O. $\dfrac{3}{4} = \dfrac{x}{30}$

V. 20 is what percent of 40?

R. 45 is what percent of 60?

H. 33 is what percent of 75?

D. 12 is what percent of 90?

E. 92 is what percent of 200?

S. 5 is what percent of 8?

The Erie Canal, which was completed in 1825, links Lake Erie in the west to the

___	___	___	___	___	___		___	___	___	___	___
44%	15	13.$\overline{3}$%	62.5%	22.5	1.5		75%	28	50%	46%	75%

in the east. At the time of its completion, some called it the Eighth Wonder of the World because of its ingenuity in engineering.

Solve each problem.

1. 24 is what percent of 30?

2. 15 is what percent of 60?

3. 25 is what percent of 50?

4. 95 is what percent of 95?

5. 18 is what percent of 24?

6. 72 is what percent of 80?

7. 44 is what percent of 55?

8. 10 is what percent of 30?

9. 125 is what percent of 150?

10. 80 is what percent of 60?

11. 92 is what percent of 138?

12. 54 is what percent of 60?

13. 9 is what percent of 10?

14. 20.2 is what percent of 10?

15. 4.8 is what percent of 6?

16. 10.5 is what percent of 12?

Finding a number when the percent is Known

All percent problems can be expressed in the format "this number is some percent of that number." You can use this format to set up a proportion to help you find a number when the percent is known.

Example 1: 40% of what number is 10?

- ◆ If 10 is 40% of some number, you must find that number.

- ◆ Write an equation. Use x to represent the number you are trying to find. $10 = 0.4 \times x$ (Remember that the word *is* in mathematics means "equals" and the word *of* indicates multiplication. Also remember that $40\% = 0.40 = 0.4$.)

- ◆ Write the new equation. $10 = 0.4x$

- ◆ Solve the equation by dividing both sides by 0.4

$$\frac{10}{0.4} = \frac{0.4x}{0.4}$$
$$x = 25$$

- ◆ 40% of 25 is 10.

Example 2: 14 is 25% of what number?

- ◆ If 14 is 25% of some number, you must find that number.

- ◆ Write an equation. $14 = 0.25 \times x$

- ◆ Write the new equation. $14 = 0.25x$

- ◆ Solve the equation by dividing both sides by 0.25.

$$\frac{14}{0.25} = \frac{0.25x}{0.25}$$
$$x = 56$$

- ◆ 25% of 56 is 14.

Example 3: $33\frac{1}{3}\%$ of what number is 30?

- ◆ If 30 is $33\frac{1}{3}\%$ of some number, you must find that number. In this example, let n represent the number you are trying to find.

- Change $33\frac{1}{3}\%$ to a fraction. $33\frac{1}{3}\% = \frac{100}{3} \times \frac{1}{100} = \frac{1}{3}$

- Write an equation. $30 = \frac{1}{3}n$ (Remember that $\frac{1}{3}n$ is the same as $\frac{1}{3} \times n$.)

- Solve for n by dividing both sides of the equation by $\frac{1}{3}$. $30 \div \frac{1}{3} = \frac{1}{3}n \div \frac{1}{3}$

- Remember that when dividing by a fraction, you must use its reciprocal and change the division sign to multiplication.

$$\frac{30}{1} \times \frac{3}{1} = \frac{1}{3}n \times \frac{3}{1}$$
$$90 = n$$

- $33\frac{1}{3}\%$ of 90 = 30.

EXERCISE 6·5

Solve. Write the letter of the problem in the space above its answer at the end of the exercise to complete the sentence. Some answers will be used twice.

A. 50% of what number is 9?

I. 72% of what number is 36?

E. 56 is 80% of what number?

U. $33\frac{1}{3}\%$ of what number is 5?

T. 25% of what number is 15?

R. 56% of what number is 42?

B. 1 is 5% of what number?

M. $83\frac{1}{3}\%$ of what number is 35?

H. 20% of what number is 6?

N. 18 is 15% of what number?

30	18	75	75	50	70	60

60	15	20	42	18	120

escaped from slavery in 1849. Afterward,

she undertook 20 rescue missions in which she led slaves in the South to freedom in the North. For her efforts, she was given the nickname "Moses."

EXERCISE 6·6

Solve.

1. 60% of what number is 30?

2. 75% of what number is 60?

3. 22% of what number is 7.7?

4. 41% of what number is 20.5?

5. 27 is 90% of what number?

6. 85% of what number is 61.2?

7. 2% of what number is 4?

8. 15 is 150% of what number?

9. 65% of what number is 45.5?

10. 37.5% of what number is 33.75?

11. $66\frac{2}{3}\%$ of what number is 33?

12. 125% of what number is 10?

13. 3.8 is 19% of what number?

14. 105% of what number is 12.6?

15. $16\frac{2}{3}\%$ of what number is 24?

16. 213.75 is 95% of what number?

EXERCISE 6·7

Solve.

1. What is 15% of 35?

2. 60% of what number is 24?

3. 40 is what percent of 40?

4. 52% of what number is 42.64?

5. What is 47% of 50?

6. 35 is what percent of 70?

7. 112 is what percent of 200?

8. 200% of what number is 8?

9. What is 75% of 12?

10. 50 is what percent of 60?

11. 2 is what percent of 5?

12. 3 is what percent of 150?

13. What is 9% of 11?

14. $44\frac{4}{9}$% of what number is 4?

15. 149% of what number is 141.55?

16. What is $33\frac{1}{3}$% of 36?

Markups, markdowns, and sales tax

Many real-life problems involve percents. Some common examples are markups, markdowns, and sales tax. A markup means that an item is sold at a higher price than it was originally purchased for. A markdown means that an item is sold at a reduced price. A markdown is the same as a sale. A sales tax is a tax added to the cost of an item upon its purchase.

Markups

Example 1: A shoe store uses a 30% markup on cost. Find the selling price for a pair of shoes that costs the store $15.

♦ The markup means that the shoe store will charge an additional 30% of the original cost of the shoes. First find 30% of $15. 0.30 × $15 = $4.50

- ♦ $4.50 is the amount added to the original cost of $15. Add to find the total cost of the pair of shoes. $4.50 + $15 = $19.50

- ♦ The shoe store will charge $19.50 for the pair of shoes.

Example 2: A computer store buys a printer from its wholesaler for $40. The computer store sells the same printer for $75. What is the markup rate?

- ♦ Find the difference between the selling price and the original price. $75 − $40 = $35

- ♦ Find what percent $35 is of $40. Set up a proportion to solve this problem. Use 35 as the part and 40 as the whole. Use x to represent the unknown percent. $\frac{35}{40} = \frac{x}{100}$

- ♦ Solve the proportion by cross-multiplying. $35 \times 100 = 40 \times x$

- ♦ Write the new equation. $3{,}500 = 40x$

- ♦ Divide both sides of the equation by 40.

$$\frac{3{,}500}{40} = \frac{40x}{40}$$
$$x = 87.5\%$$

- ♦ The markup rate is 87.5%.

Markdowns

Example 1: An item was originally priced at $65. It was marked down 25%. What is the sale price?

- ♦ Find 25% of $65. This is the amount of money that is taken off the original price. $0.25 \times \$65 = \$16.25$

- ♦ Because $16.25 is taken off the original price, subtract $16.25 from the original price to find the sale price. $65 − $16.25 = $48.75

- ♦ The sale price is $48.75.

Example 2: An item that regularly sells for $150 is discounted to $99. What is the discount rate? (A discount rate is the same as the rate of a markdown.)

- ♦ Find the difference between the original price and the discounted price. $150 − $99 = $51

- ♦ Write a proportion to find what percent $51 is of $150. $\frac{51}{150} = \frac{x}{100}$

- ♦ Solve the proportion by cross-multiplying. $51 \times 100 = 150 \times x$

- ♦ Write the new equation. $5{,}100 = 150x$

◆ Divide both sides of the equation by 150.

$$\frac{5,100}{150} = \frac{150x}{150}$$
$$x = 34$$

◆ The discount rate is 34%.

Sales tax

Example 1: The cost for a dinner, before sales tax was added, was $45. The sales tax was 7.5%. How much was the total bill?

◆ Find 7.5% of $45. This number represents the amount of tax added to the check.
0.075 × $45 = $3.375

◆ Add the sales tax to the original amount. $45 + $3.375 = $48.375

◆ Round your answer to the nearest cent. The total bill is $48.38.

Example 2: While on vacation, Tonya bought a souvenir for $20. She was charged $22. What was the percent of sales tax?

◆ Find the difference between the original amount and the total amount Tonya was charged. $22 – $20 = $2

◆ Set up a proportion to find what percent $2 is of $20. $\frac{2}{20} = \frac{x}{100}$

◆ Write an equivalent fraction to find the unknown percent. $\frac{2}{20} = \frac{2 \times 5}{20 \times 5} = \frac{10}{100}$

◆ The sales tax is 10%.

EXERCISE
6·8

Solve each problem. Write the letter of the problem in the space above its answer at the end of the exercise to complete the sentence. Some answers will be used twice. Round answers that are in money to the nearest cent, if necessary.

A. A jewelry store uses a markup rate of 45%. Find the selling price of a necklace that the store purchased for $125.

G. An office supply store uses a markup rate of 20%. Find the selling price of a desk lamp that the store purchased for $15.

O. A sporting goods shop pays its wholesaler $10 for a workout T-shirt. The shop charges its customers $15 for the T-shirt. What is the markup rate?

T. A video game store pays its wholesaler $40 for a video game. The store charges its customers $65 for the video game. What is the markup rate?

F. A department store had a 40% off sale. A sweater originally cost $75. What was the sale price?

L. A grocery store is selling candy for 50% off the original price. The candy originally cost $3.50. What is the sale price?

I. A CD is on sale for $8. It originally cost $12. What is the discount rate?

N. A TV is on sale for $350. It originally cost $500. What is the discount rate?

U. A dinner bill was subject to a sales tax of 6.5%. The bill before the tax was $55. Find the amount of the sales tax.

S. The tax on a plumber's bill is 3.5%. The bill was $99 before tax. What is the total bill including the tax?

E. You were charged $53 for an original bill of $50. What is the sales tax rate?

The ___ ___ _____ ____ _____ ____   ____ ____
     $1.75 6% $181.25 $18 $3.58 6%   50% $45

___ _____ _____ _____ _____ ____ _____ was formed after
30% $181.25 62.5% 33.$\overline{3}$% 50% 30% $102.47

World War I in hopes of avoiding another world war.

Complete each chart. Round prices to the nearest cent, if necessary.

	Original price	Markup	Markup price
1.	$20	30%	
2.	$100		$114
3.	$40		$44
4.	$58.25	40%	

	Original price	Markdown	Sale price
5.	$72	25%	
6.	$21		$14
7.	$62.80	60%	
8.	$90		$63

	Original price	Sales tax	Total price
9.	$12.50	2%	
10.	$28		$29.40
11.	$45.99	6%	
12.	$75		$78

Percent of increase and decrease

An increase and percent of increase are related. An increase is a number, whereas a percent of increase is a ratio of the increase to the original amount.

Likewise, a decrease and percent of decrease are related. A decrease is a number, whereas a percent of decrease is a ratio of the decrease to the original amount.

Problems involving the percent of increase and decrease can be solved using the formulas below.

Percent of Increase: $\dfrac{\text{increase}}{\text{original amount}} = \dfrac{n}{100}$

Percent of Decrease: $\dfrac{\text{decrease}}{\text{original amount}} = \dfrac{n}{100}$

Example 1: James went on a diet to reach a lower weight class for wrestling. His weight dropped from 180 to 165 pounds. By what percent did his weight decrease?

- ◆ Find the decrease by subtracting the new weight from the original weight.
  180 − 165 = 15

- ◆ Substitute the values into the formula for finding the percent of decrease. $\frac{15}{180} = \frac{n}{100}$

- ◆ Solve the proportion by cross-multiplying. 15 × 100 = 180 × n

- ◆ Write the new equation. 1,500 = 180n

- ◆ Divide both sides of the equation by 180.

$$\frac{1,500}{180} = \frac{180n}{180}$$
$$n = 8.\overline{3}\%$$

- ◆ James's weight decreased by 8.$\overline{3}$%.

Example 2: The town where Mika was born had a population of 2,500 people. Ten years later, the population of the town was 2,675 people. What was the percent of increase?

- ◆ Find the increase by subtracting the original population from the new population.
  2,675 − 2,500 = 175

- ◆ Substitute the values into the formula for finding the percent of increase. $\frac{175}{2,500} = \frac{n}{100}$

- ◆ Solve the proportion by cross-multiplying. 175 × 100 = 2,500 × n

- ◆ Write the new equation. 17,500 = 2,500n

- ◆ Divide both sides of the equation by 2,500.

$$\frac{17,500}{2,500} = \frac{2,500n}{2,500}$$
$$n = 7$$

- ◆ The population increased by 7%.

EXERCISE
6·10

Solve each problem. Write the letter of the problem in the space above its answer at the end of the exercise to complete the sentence. Some answers will be used more than once.

L. The annual dues for the cooking club increased from $10 to $15. What is the percent of increase?

U. Ron's salary increased from $15 per hour to $18 per hour. What was the percent of increase?

A.   A CD was originally priced at $12. It went on sale for $10. What was the percent of decrease?

N.   The price of avocados decreased from $1.50 to $1. What was the percent of decrease?

E.   Lena's math average increased from 80% to 90%. What was the percent of increase?

C.   The temperature dropped from 80 degrees during the day to 65 degrees at night. What was the percent of decrease?

S.   The Hendersons expanded the area of their garden. The garden was originally 100 square feet. Now it is 175 square feet. What was the percent of increase?

P.   A bus company had 24 local routes. The company eliminated 22 of the routes, leaving only 2 local routes. By what percent did the number of local routes decrease?

T.   Jackie decreased her time for running a mile from 8 minutes to 6 minutes. What was the percent of decrease?

O.   Tim's new house is 25 miles from his job. His old house was 13 miles from his job. What was the percent of increase?

___ ___ ___ ___ ___ ___ ___ ___ ___
18.75% 12.5% 50% 50% 20% 50% 48% 75% 12.5%

is a type of carbohydrate found in ___ ___ ___ ___ ___ ___.
91.$\overline{6}$% 50% 16.$\overline{6}$% 33.$\overline{3}$% 25% 75%

It is the most abundant organic compound on earth.

Find the percent of increase or decrease for each item below.

	Item	Original amount	New amount	Percent of increase or decrease
1.	T-shirt	$25	$30	
2.	Coffee	$2.50	$5.00	
3.	Science test average	90%	88%	
4.	Interest rate	5%	4.5%	
5.	Electric bill	$90	$82	
6.	Gasoline	$3.00	$3.90	
7.	Blue jeans	$80	$50	
8.	Cell phone bill	$100	$120	
9.	Swimming 1 lap	1 minute	45 seconds	
10.	Running 100 meters	15 seconds	12 seconds	
11.	Heart rate	80 beats per minute	68 beats per minute	
12.	Volume	60 mL	100 mL	
13.	Jumping jacks per minute	45	68	
14.	Rainfall	4 inches	3 inches	
15.	Temperature	32 degrees	40 degrees	
16.	Altitude	750 feet	900 feet	

Simple interest

Interest is a charge for a loan, based on the percentage of the amount borrowed. You can also earn interest for some investments, for example, money in a bank account. The amount of interest you pay or earn depends on the interest rate, the amount of money (principal) borrowed or invested, and the length of time the money is borrowed or invested.

Simple interest is the easiest type of interest to compute. To compute simple interest, use the formula $I = Prt$, where I is the interest paid or earned, P is the principal (the amount of money borrowed or invested), r is the interest rate, and t is the time, expressed in years, that the principal amount is owed or invested.

Example 1: Find the amount of interest on $5,000 invested at a 4% interest rate for 3 years.

◆ Use the formula $I = Prt$ and substitute the value for each variable.
    $P = \$5,000$
    $r = 0.04$ (Remember to convert a percent to a decimal before
        performing any calculations.)
    $t = 3$

◆ Multiply. $I = \$5,000 \times 0.04 \times 3$ $I = \$600$

◆ $600 interest is earned.

Example 2: Sanjay borrowed $100 from his brother, who charged him interest. The amount of interest Sanjay paid at the end of 6 months was $1.50. What was the interest rate?

◆ Use the formula $I = Prt$ and substitute the value for each variable.
    $I = \$1.50$
    $P = \$100$
    $t = 0.5$ because 6 months is 0.5 year.
    $\$1.50 = \$100 \times r \times 0.5$

◆ $\$1.50 = \$50r$ because $\$100 \times 0.5 = \$50$.

◆ Solve for r by dividing both sides of the equation by 50.

$$\frac{1.50}{50} = \frac{50r}{50}$$
$$r = 0.03$$

◆ Convert the decimal to a percent. The interest rate was 3%.

Solve each problem. Write the letter of the problem in the space above its answer at the end of the exercise to complete the sentence. Some answers will be used twice.

M. Damon borrowed $15,000 to buy a car. The interest rate for his loan is 5% for 5 years. How much will he pay in interest?

U. Frank placed $500 in a savings account at the bank. His account earns 2.5% interest. If he does not take any money out, how much money will he have in his account after 4 years? (Hint: Add the interest earned to the principal.)

E. Tara borrowed $50 from her mom. Her mom told her that she has to pay 1% interest on the loan. How much interest will Tara pay after 1 year?

I. Peter wants to earn $1,200 in 5 years from an account that earns 4% interest. How much will he have to invest?

P. Madeline placed $2,000 in a bank account. She earned 4.5% on this investment. She did not take any money out and earned $450 in interest. How many years did she leave her money in the account?

N. Olivia borrowed $750 to buy a new computer. She will pay 2.5% interest for 4 years. How much money will she pay in interest?

T. Caroline earned $1,155 on an investment. Her investment had an interest rate of 5.5% and she left the principal in the account for 7 years. How much was her original investment?

O. Sammi invested $3,000 in a bank account. She did not take any of the money out of the account. After 18 months, she had $3,225 in the account. What interest rate did she earn?

R. Rico borrowed $10,000 to help pay for college. He was charged an interest rate of 5.5%. How much interest will Rico pay after 5 years?

C. Joey deposited $1,500 in a savings account in the bank. He did not take any money out of the account. After 6 months, he earned $18.75 in interest. What was the interest rate?

D. Kayla earned $90 in interest on her original investment of $600. The interest rate she received was 7.5%. How many years was her money invested?

S. Jeremy bought an entertainment center for his home. He borrowed $10,000 at an interest rate of 5%. How much interest will he pay at the end of 5 years?

___ ___ ___ ___ ___ ___ ___ ___
2.5%   5% $3,750   5   5% $550 $75   2

___ ___ ___ ___ ___ ___ ___ ___ is earned on both the
$6,000 $75 $3,000 $0.50 $2,750 $0.50 $2,500 $3,000

principal and previous interest earned. Over time, these investments earn much more than investments that earn simple interest.

EXERCISE
6·13

Complete the chart by filling in the missing values.

	Principal	Interest rate	Time (in years)	Interest earned
1.	$2,000	4%	2	
2.	$500	3.5%	7	
3.	$1,500	2.5%		$375
4.	$5,000		5	$1,500
5.		5%	8	$240
6.	$700	7%	4	
7.	$8,575	2%		$514.50

	Principal	Interest rate	Time (in years)	Interest earned
8.		4.5%	12	$1,687.50
10.	$18,000		2	$2,880
11.	$7,500	6.25%		$1,875
12.	$1,000	3.5%	5.5	
13.		6%	3.5	$120.75
14.	$1,250		4	$195
15.	$4,550	7.5%	8	
16.		2.75%	9	$49,500

Answer Key

1   Understanding fractional relationships

1·1   1. $\frac{1}{5}$ 2. 1 or $\frac{2}{2}$ 3. $\frac{1}{3}$ 4. $\frac{4}{10}$ or $\frac{2}{5}$ 5. $\frac{1}{2}$ 6. $\frac{6}{9}$ or $\frac{2}{3}$ 7. $\frac{2}{3}$ 8. $\frac{3}{4}$ 9 to 16. Answers will vary. The denominator shows the number of equal parts that make up 1 whole. The numerator indicates the number of equal parts that are shaded.

1·2   1.

9.
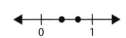

2.

10.
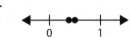

3.

11.
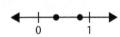

4.
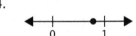

12.
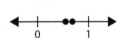

5.

13.
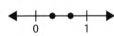

6.

14.

7.

15.

8.

16.

1·3   C. 45   N. 30   A. 18   R. 35   M. 20   O. 51   I. 84   S. 72   E. 100   L. 42   U. 60
T. 144   Transcontinental

1·4 1. 15 2. 24 3. 24 4. 42 5. 63 6. 40 7. 30 8. 18 9. $2 \times 3 \times 5 \times 7 = 210$

10. $2 \times 5^2 = 50$ 11. $2^2 \times 3 \times 5 = 60$ 12. $2^2 \times 7 = 28$ 13. $2^2 \times 3^2 \times 5 = 180$

14. $2^2 \times 11 \times 13 = 572$ 15. $2^2 \times 3^2 = 72$ 16. $2^3 \times 3^2 \times 5 = 360$

1·5 I. $\frac{20}{25}$ A. $\frac{24}{64}$ G. $\frac{15}{18}$ T. $\frac{28}{36}$ Y. $\frac{1}{8}$ H. $\frac{1}{2}$ D. $\frac{6}{7}$ L. $\frac{3}{4}$
Daylight

1·6 1. Yes; multiply by 4. 2. Yes; divide by 4. 3. Yes; multiply by 5. 4. No; fractions will vary.
A possible answer is $\frac{14}{28}$. 5. No; fractions will vary. A possible answer is
$\frac{5}{6}$. 6. Yes; multiply by 12. 7. Yes; divide by 3. 8. No; fractions will vary. A possible answer is
$\frac{9}{10}$. 9. $\frac{9}{18}$ 10. $\frac{3}{5}$ 11. $\frac{18}{42}$ 12. $\frac{7}{14}$ 13. $\frac{15}{27}$ 14. $\frac{1}{8}$ 15. $\frac{5}{10}$ 16. $\frac{56}{64}$

1·7 1. >, I 2. >, K 3. >, D 4. <, R 5. <, C 6. =, Y 7. >, L 8. >, O 9. >, H Old Hickory

1·8 1. > 2. > 3. > 4. > 5. < 6. < 7. > 8. < 9. < 10. < 11. > 12. > 13. < 14. < 15. < 16. >

1·9 1. >, A 2. >, T 3. <, L 4. >, R 5. <, I 6. =, U 7. >, O 8. >, G 9. =, C 10. <, S 11. >, N coal, oil,
. . . natural gas

1·10 1. > 2. = 3. > 4. > 5. < 6. < 7. < 8. = 9. < 10. > 11. > 12. > 13. > 14. < 15. < 16. <

1·11 1. $\frac{1}{2}, \frac{5}{8}, \frac{3}{4}$; L 2. $\frac{5}{6}, \frac{5}{8}, \frac{7}{12}$; R 3. $\frac{1}{2}, \frac{2}{3}, \frac{7}{8}$; O 4. $\frac{11}{14}, \frac{4}{7}, \frac{1}{2}$; E 5. $\frac{6}{15}, \frac{7}{10}, \frac{4}{5}$; C 6. $\frac{1}{2}, \frac{4}{6}, \frac{3}{4}$; Y
Eye color

1·12 1. $\frac{1}{4}, \frac{3}{5}, \frac{5}{6}$ 2. $\frac{2}{5}, \frac{2}{4}, \frac{4}{6}$ 3. $\frac{1}{3}, \frac{4}{10}, \frac{4}{5}$ 4. $\frac{1}{18}, \frac{2}{9}, \frac{1}{3}$ 5. $\frac{1}{6}, \frac{3}{8}, \frac{5}{12}$ 6. $\frac{3}{7}, \frac{4}{6}, \frac{10}{14}$ 7. $\frac{5}{9}, \frac{7}{12}, \frac{3}{4}$ 8. $\frac{3}{5}, \frac{13}{20},$
$\frac{7}{8}$ 9. $\frac{10}{12}, \frac{3}{4}, \frac{5}{9}$ 10. $\frac{5}{12}, \frac{2}{6}, \frac{3}{10}$ 11. $\frac{12}{16}, \frac{45}{64}, \frac{4}{8}$ 12. $\frac{12}{13}, \frac{4}{5}, \frac{14}{21}$ 13. $\frac{2}{6}, \frac{3}{10}, \frac{2}{7}$ 14. $\frac{5}{6}, \frac{4}{9}, \frac{7}{18}$ 15. $\frac{11}{14},$
$\frac{6}{8}, \frac{3}{7}$ 16. $\frac{11}{12}, \frac{27}{30}, \frac{3}{4}$

1·13 R. 6 S. 31 M. 14 C. 10 D. 5 U. 12 H. 25 T. 3 E. 11 L. 74 O. 1 N. 30
Chromosomes . . . nucleus

1·14 1. 2 2. 9 3. 5 4. 13 5. 12 6. 2 7. 9 8. 1 9. 2 10. 4 11. 7 12. 2 13. 4 14. 2 15. 1 16. 5

1·15 H. $\frac{1}{2}$ E. $\frac{4}{5}$ F. $\frac{1}{3}$ I. $\frac{7}{9}$ J. $\frac{2}{3}$ P. $\frac{7}{11}$ O. $\frac{3}{5}$ S. $\frac{22}{25}$ N. $\frac{14}{15}$ C. $\frac{5}{6}$
Chief Joseph

1·16 1. $\frac{1}{2}$ 2. $\frac{3}{7}$ 3. $\frac{1}{3}$ 4. $\frac{2}{3}$ 5. $\frac{1}{4}$ 6. $\frac{8}{11}$ 7. $\frac{1}{5}$ 8. $\frac{5}{8}$ 9. $\frac{5}{8}$ 10. $\frac{5}{6}$ 11. $\frac{7}{8}$ 12. $\frac{1}{6}$ 13. $\frac{6}{7}$ 14. $\frac{4}{9}$ 15. $\frac{7}{19}$
16. $\frac{9}{10}$

1·17 A. $4\frac{4}{5}$ N. $5\frac{2}{3}$ I. $7\frac{1}{2}$ T. $4\frac{1}{4}$ C. 7 O. $8\frac{5}{6}$ R. $\frac{19}{4}$ S. $\frac{19}{3}$ M. $\frac{13}{2}$ L. $\frac{50}{7}$ E. $\frac{69}{8}$ P. $\frac{16}{3}$
Emancipation Proclamation

1·18 1. $3\frac{3}{4}$ 2. $2\frac{2}{3}$ 3. $5\frac{2}{5}$ 4. $5\frac{1}{10}$ 5. 6 6. $3\frac{2}{3}$ 7. $6\frac{1}{8}$ 8. 10 9. $\frac{19}{5}$ 10. $\frac{11}{6}$ 11. $\frac{13}{3}$ 12. $\frac{79}{10}$ 13. $\frac{50}{9}$
14. $\frac{35}{8}$ 15. $\frac{76}{11}$ 16. $\frac{73}{9}$

2 Operations with fractions

2·1 1. 1 2. $\frac{1}{2}$ 3. 0 4. $\frac{1}{2}$ 5. 0 6. $\frac{1}{2}$ 7. $1\frac{1}{2}$ 8. 0 9. $\frac{1}{2}$ 10. $\frac{1}{2}$ 11. 0 12. 1 13. 0 14. $1\frac{1}{2}$ 15. 2 16. 1

2·2 1. $\frac{1}{2}$ 2. $\frac{3}{5}$ 3. $\frac{1}{2}$ 4. $\frac{1}{3}$ 5. $\frac{4}{7}$ 6. $\frac{10}{11}$ 7. $\frac{2}{5}$ 8. 1 9. $\frac{1}{3}$ 10. $\frac{4}{9}$ 11. $\frac{4}{13}$ 12. $1\frac{1}{5}$ 13. $\frac{1}{17}$ 14. $\frac{8}{13}$ 15. $\frac{8}{9}$
16. $1\frac{1}{3}$

2·3 E. $\frac{8}{9}$ I. $\frac{17}{40}$ P. $1\frac{1}{12}$ N. $1\frac{13}{30}$ A. $1\frac{8}{33}$ M. $1\frac{11}{24}$ J. $1\frac{1}{45}$ S. $\frac{11}{28}$
Japanese

2·4 1. $\frac{5}{8}$ 2. $\frac{9}{10}$ 3. $1\frac{5}{18}$ 4. $\frac{17}{18}$ 5. $\frac{25}{42}$ 6. $\frac{19}{22}$ 7. $1\frac{13}{44}$ 8. $1\frac{13}{40}$ 9. $\frac{19}{24}$ 10. $1\frac{4}{21}$ 11. $1\frac{1}{27}$ 12. $\frac{34}{45}$ 13. $\frac{17}{60}$
14. $\frac{5}{16}$ 15. $1\frac{8}{39}$ 16. $1\frac{4}{7}$

2·5 O. $\frac{3}{8}$ S. $\frac{1}{5}$ N. $\frac{23}{42}$ T. $\frac{19}{40}$ U. $\frac{13}{20}$ L. $\frac{9}{35}$ I. $\frac{1}{6}$ C. $\frac{4}{15}$
Constitution

2·6 1. $\frac{5}{14}$ 2. $\frac{7}{18}$ 3. $\frac{1}{2}$ 4. $\frac{3}{4}$ 5. $\frac{4}{9}$ 6. $\frac{1}{12}$ 7. $\frac{5}{12}$ 8. $\frac{1}{18}$ 9. $\frac{3}{10}$ 10. $\frac{1}{4}$ 11. $\frac{19}{45}$ 12. $\frac{23}{28}$ 13. $\frac{13}{28}$ 14. $\frac{11}{40}$
15. $\frac{13}{24}$ 16. $\frac{13}{33}$

2·7 1. 4 2. $1\frac{1}{7}$ 3. $2\frac{2}{5}$ 4. $9\frac{1}{3}$ 5. $2\frac{1}{3}$ 6. $2\frac{1}{5}$ 7. 6 8. $8\frac{1}{4}$ 9. $1\frac{1}{4}$ 10. $2\frac{8}{9}$ 11. $1\frac{1}{9}$ 12. $3\frac{1}{2}$ 13. $10\frac{4}{5}$
14. $8\frac{4}{7}$ 15. 4 16. $8\frac{9}{13}$

2·8 A. $4\frac{1}{2}$ E. $4\frac{1}{14}$ I. $6\frac{5}{18}$ R. $2\frac{23}{36}$ G. $10\frac{34}{63}$ T. $2\frac{3}{28}$ N. $9\frac{7}{12}$ B. $10\frac{51}{55}$
Great Britain

2·9 1. $3\frac{5}{6}$ 2. $5\frac{7}{24}$ 3. $6\frac{4}{5}$ 4. $6\frac{4}{21}$ 5. $5\frac{7}{18}$ 6. $12\frac{29}{30}$ 7. $5\frac{9}{16}$ 8. $4\frac{31}{45}$ 9. $6\frac{31}{35}$ 10. $5\frac{24}{55}$ 11. $4\frac{9}{40}$ 12. $14\frac{5}{6}$
13. $4\frac{2}{3}$ 14. $18\frac{5}{21}$ 15. $13\frac{5}{21}$ 16. $13\frac{13}{63}$

2·10 R. $2\frac{9}{16}$ O. $2\frac{3}{10}$ E. $1\frac{11}{18}$ I. $3\frac{1}{12}$ T. $2\frac{1}{8}$ P. $1\frac{2}{45}$ N. $1\frac{2}{7}$ S. $3\frac{1}{2}$
preposition

2·11 1. $1\frac{3}{10}$ 2. $1\frac{2}{9}$ 3. $1\frac{2}{21}$ 4. $5\frac{11}{24}$ 5. $6\frac{1}{8}$ 6. $5\frac{5}{24}$ 7. $5\frac{1}{12}$ 8. $7\frac{8}{21}$ 9. $1\frac{13}{24}$ 10. 2 11. $2\frac{3}{10}$ 12. $6\frac{19}{30}$
13. $2\frac{4}{15}$ 14. $1\frac{1}{18}$ 15. $4\frac{1}{30}$ 16. $9\frac{13}{56}$

2·12 M. $2\frac{17}{20}$ O. $4\frac{13}{24}$ E. $2\frac{13}{18}$ W. $3\frac{5}{12}$ A. $4\frac{7}{18}$ S. $2\frac{1}{5}$ J. $3\frac{23}{40}$ I. $4\frac{1}{12}$ D. $3\frac{1}{3}$ N. $1\frac{25}{28}$
James Madison

2·13 1. $1\frac{13}{20}$ 2. $1\frac{2}{3}$ 3. $1\frac{2}{3}$ 4. $4\frac{23}{30}$ 5. $2\frac{19}{28}$ 6. $\frac{29}{40}$ 7. $4\frac{3}{4}$ 8. $6\frac{11}{14}$ 9. $5\frac{11}{12}$ 10. $6\frac{32}{55}$ 11. $3\frac{1}{2}$ 12. $1\frac{11}{24}$
13. $4\frac{43}{72}$ 14. $4\frac{4}{9}$ 15. $4\frac{9}{20}$ 16. $8\frac{3}{5}$

2·14 Y. $\frac{4}{15}$ A. $\frac{8}{25}$ N. $\frac{1}{16}$ E. $\frac{1}{4}$ D. $\frac{8}{45}$ I. $\frac{7}{20}$ C. $\frac{1}{56}$ R. $\frac{3}{5}$ G. $\frac{3}{25}$ L. $\frac{1}{8}$
dry-cleaning

2·15 1. $\frac{8}{35}$ 2. $\frac{1}{4}$ 3. $\frac{1}{3}$ 4. $\frac{2}{9}$ 5. $\frac{7}{12}$ 6. $\frac{1}{9}$ 7. $\frac{7}{24}$ 8. $\frac{9}{22}$ 9. $\frac{3}{7}$ 10. $\frac{2}{5}$ 11. $\frac{1}{8}$ 12. $\frac{2}{3}$ 13. $\frac{3}{8}$ 14. $\frac{1}{10}$
15. $\frac{2}{11}$ 16. $\frac{1}{12}$

2·16   R. $\frac{18}{25}$ B. $8\frac{7}{16}$ I. $\frac{5}{12}$ A. $2\frac{2}{5}$ E. $1\frac{1}{5}$ G. $2\frac{2}{3}$ D. 2   T. $9\frac{1}{5}$ M. $2\frac{1}{4}$ S. $10\frac{15}{16}$

Sesame Street . . . Big Bird

2·17   1. $1\frac{1}{4}$ 2. $9\frac{1}{2}$ 3. $2\frac{23}{36}$ 4. $10\frac{1}{5}$ 5. $1\frac{1}{5}$ 6. 6   7. $48\frac{5}{42}$ 8. $2\frac{4}{5}$ 9. $13\frac{1}{15}$ 10. 3   11. $4\frac{3}{8}$ 12. $7\frac{7}{9}$

13. $10\frac{1}{2}$ 14. $64\frac{3}{5}$ 15. $16\frac{8}{15}$ 16. 45

2·18   M. $2\frac{3}{11}$ A. $\frac{8}{15}$ K. $\frac{14}{15}$ R. $\frac{15}{16}$ S. $1\frac{1}{2}$ E. $\frac{9}{10}$ N. $\frac{4}{15}$ D. $\frac{2}{9}$

Sneakers . . . Keds

2·19   1. $\frac{5}{14}$ 2. $\frac{6}{7}$ 3. $2\frac{1}{2}$ 4. $2\frac{2}{3}$ 5. $1\frac{1}{63}$ 6. $1\frac{1}{24}$ 7. $\frac{5}{6}$ 8. 1   9. $4\frac{4}{5}$ 10. 3   11. $4\frac{1}{2}$ 12. $2\frac{1}{6}$ 13. $\frac{3}{25}$

14. $1\frac{5}{9}$ 15. 1   16. $2\frac{2}{11}$

2·20   I. 1   A. $\frac{2}{15}$ S. $2\frac{4}{9}$ N. $22\frac{1}{2}$ D. 32   O. $\frac{7}{9}$ F. $\frac{1}{7}$ L. $3\frac{5}{17}$

Indiana . . . Land of Indians

2·21   1. $3\frac{3}{4}$ 2. $\frac{44}{51}$ 3. $1\frac{13}{36}$ 4. $\frac{9}{46}$ 5. 9   6. $1\frac{23}{32}$ 7. $1\frac{1}{32}$ 8. 20   9. $\frac{5}{18}$ 10. $5\frac{19}{26}$ 11. $2\frac{25}{28}$ 12. $1\frac{11}{12}$

13. 21   14. $3\frac{1}{3}$ 15. 12   16. $2\frac{47}{95}$

2·22   1. $9\frac{17}{20}$ 2. $1\frac{8}{15}$ 3. 1   4. $3\frac{1}{18}$ 5. $2\frac{9}{10}$ 6. $1\frac{13}{20}$ 7. $2\frac{8}{21}$ 8. $2\frac{17}{84}$ 9. $\frac{7}{12}$ 10. $3\frac{2}{7}$ 11. $1\frac{11}{24}$ 12. $4\frac{7}{30}$

13. $\frac{1}{24}$ 14. $10\frac{14}{15}$ 15. $8\frac{1}{3}$ 16. $\frac{9}{44}$

3   Connecting fractions and decimals

3·1   1. 8 tenths   2. 2 hundred-thousandths   3. 4 tens   4. 0 hundredths   5. One and eighty-five hundredths   6. Four hundred two thousandths   7. Twelve and three tenths   8. One and thirty-four thousandths   9. 3.5   10. 11.75   11. 0.345   12. 0.0007

3·2   1. $10 \times 10 = 100$ 2. 10   3. $10 \times 10 \times 10 \times 10 = 10{,}000$ 4. $\frac{1}{10 \times 10} = \frac{1}{100}$ 5. $\frac{1}{10 \times 10 \times 10} = \frac{1}{1{,}000}$ 6. $10 \times 10 \times 10 = 1{,}000$ 7. $\frac{1}{10}$ 8. $10 \times 10 \times 10 \times 10 \times 10 = 100{,}000$ 9. $\frac{1}{10 \times 10 \times 10 \times 10 \times 10 \times 10} = \frac{1}{1{,}000{,}000}$
10. $10 \times 10 \times 10 \times 10 \times 10 \times 10 = 1{,}000{,}000$ 11. $10 \times 10 \times 10 \times 10 \times 10 \times 10 \times 10 \times 10 \times 10 \times 10 = 10{,}000{,}000{,}000$ 12. $\frac{1}{10 \times 10 \times 10 \times 10 \times 10 \times 10 \times 10 \times 10} = \frac{1}{100{,}000{,}000}$ 13. 1   14. $\frac{1}{10 \times 10 \times 10 \times 10} = \frac{1}{10{,}000}$
15. $10 \times 10 \times 10 \times 10 \times 10 \times 10 \times 10 = 10{,}000{,}000$ 16. $\frac{1}{10 \times 10 \times 10 \times 10 \times 10 \times 10 \times 10 \times 10 \times 10 \times 10} = \frac{1}{10{,}000{,}000{,}000}$

3·3   1. $40 + 3 + 0.8 + 0.04$ 2. $5 + 0.9 + 0.02$ 3. $500 + 1 + 0.9$ 4. $7 + 0.8 + 0.02 + 0.001$ 5. $9 + 0.3 + 0.04 + 0.009$ 6. $0.1 + 0.09 + 0.007 + 0.0005$ 7. $10 + 2 + 0.9 + 0.08 + 0.003$ 8. $100 + 4 + 0.9 + 0.08$ 9. 9.305   10. 0.145   11. 13.006   12. 67.409   13. 174.02   14. 309.84   15. 90.006   16. 240.088

3·4   E. 0.25   D. 5.5   O. 0.1   S. 0.875   I. $3.\overline{6}$ M. $0.1\overline{6}$ K. $0.5\overline{3}$ Z. $0.\overline{4}$ T. 3.08   N. $0.91\overline{6}$

time zones

3·5   1. 0.625   2. 0.6   3. 3.4   4. $0.\overline{6}$ 5. 0.3   6. 7.5625   7. 2.75   8. 0.15   9. $5.1\overline{6}$ 10. 0.2   11. $0.\overline{2}$
12. $0.4\overline{6}$ 13. $6.\overline{72}$ 14. $0.\overline{63}$ 15. $8.08\overline{3}$ 16. 4.6875

3·6 U. $\frac{9}{10}$ I. $1\frac{17}{50}$ S. $\frac{7}{20}$ N. $2\frac{1}{4}$ E. $\frac{1}{8}$ O. $4\frac{89}{100}$ C. $\frac{4}{33}$ H. $\frac{5}{9}$ R. $4\frac{19}{20}$ A. $\frac{4}{5}$

Hurricanes

3·7 1. $\frac{3}{4}$ 2. $1\frac{11}{20}$ 3. $\frac{83}{99}$ 4. $\frac{191}{200}$ 5. $1\frac{2}{5}$ 6. $3\frac{5}{9}$ 7. $3\frac{23}{25}$ 8. $\frac{12}{25}$ 9. $\frac{103}{200}$ 10. $5\frac{3}{20}$ 11. $\frac{5}{8}$ 12. $\frac{1}{5}$ 13. $2\frac{8}{9}$

14. $2\frac{24}{125}$ 15. $\frac{1}{11}$ 16. $1\frac{46}{99}$

3·8 1. 0.9 2. 0.42 3. 1.1 4. 3.19 5. 5.1 6. 2.75

7.

12.
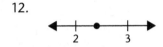

8.
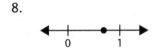

13.
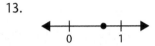

9.

14.
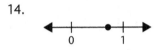

10.

15.

11.
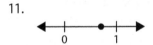

16.

3·9 1. <, I 2. <, N 3. =, A 4. >, T 5. <, H 6. >, G 7. <, M 8. =, D

Mahatma Gandhi

3·10 1. > 2. < 3. < 4. < 5. = 6. < 7. < 8. < 9. > 10. > 11. > 12. < 13. < 14. > 15. < 16. <

3·11 1. 0.99, 1.4, 1.57, 1.85, 1.9; I 2. 0.9, 0.81, 0.75, 0.45, 0.2; R 3. 0.15, 0.19, 0.22, 0.73, 1.01; A
4. 5.9, 5.5, 5.32, 4.91, 4.7; C 5. 1.95, 2.01, 2.04, 2.05, 2.4; T 6. 8.59, 8.3, 8.257, 8.25, 8.11; W
7. 0.3, 0.34, 0.44, 0.51, 0.6; E 8. 0.88, 0.808, 0.781, 0.78, 0.26; N 9. 1.08, 1.63, 1.72, 1.9, 2.1;
H 10. 1.4, 1.24, 1.044, 1.04, 1.024; G 11. 3.001, 3.002, 3.01, 3.02, 3.1; L

Great Wall . . . China

3·12 1. 0.4, 0.5, 0.7, 0.9, 1 2. 0.4, 0.42, 0.7, 0.71, 0.88 3. 1.3, 1.32, 1.55, 1.67, 1.9 4. 2.003, 2.005,
2.02, 2.04, 2.1 5. 1.08, 2.7, 3.4, 4.3, 5.1 6. 0.089, 0.799, 0.805, 0.905, 0.923 7. 2.33, 2.58, 3.75,
3.79, 4.01 8. 1.064, 1.072, 1.505, 1.55, 1.63 9. 7.51, 7.4, 7.304, 7.3, 7.062 10. 0.592, 0.491,
0.399, 0.382, 0.354 11. 5.0385, 5.0183, 5.011, 5.002, 5 12. 10.9, 10.7, 10.28, 1.08, 1.02 13. 1.94,
1.4, 1.09, 1.048, 1.028 14. 0.202, 0.2, 0.02, 0.002, 0.0002 15. 3.928, 3.22, 3.174, 3.172, 3.1
16. 8.8, 8.293, 8.29, 8.23, 8.01

4 Operations with decimals

4·1 1. 0.8 2. 1.6 3. 1.57 4. 4.10 5. 1 6. 4 7. 1.383 8. 0.929 9. 3 10. 6 11. 1 12. 0 13. 13 14. 1 15. 4 16. 13

4·2 N. 0.82 O. 4.13 L. 1.4 A. 0.59 K. 7.72 E. 2.02 T. 7.1 S. 0.62 F. 3.18 R. 8.35 V. 3.67 I. 4.82

Franklin . . . Roosevelt

4·3 1. 0.8 2. 1.67 3. 0.24 4. 0.2 5. 4.5 6. 5.73 7. 0.125 8. 7.414 9. 4.627 10. 1.998 11. 9.302 12. 0.224 13. 1.358 14. 1.8063 15. 12.993 16. 4.6143

4·4 E. 1.2 L. 0.504 O. 2.125 B. 6.46 R. 2.4 T. 0.012 A. 0.07 S. 2.7

Robert La Salle

4·5 1. 0.42 2. 0.1334 3. 0.38 4. 1.615 5. 2.1 6. 4.173 7. 3.2736 8. 1.5 9. 4.2 10. 0.2769 11. 0.66794 12. 0.001 13. 5.616 14. 14.714 15. 1.164 16. 18.36055

4·6 A. 0.5 M. 0.8 D. 0.45 R. $1.21\overline{3}$ O. 1.955 S. 9.1 G. 4.35 N. 6.575

Roman gods

4·7 1. 2.1 2. 0.4 3. 0.7 4. 0.3 5. 2.1 6. 0.615 7. 2.75 8. 0.5725 9. 2.155 10. $2.23\overline{6}$ 11. $1.64\overline{3}$ 12. 16.5 13. 10.1 14. 8.475 15. $1.01\overline{5}$ 16. $2.80\overline{6}$

4·8 S. 16.3 N. 4.9 U. 5.175 T. $14.\overline{12}$ P. $20.0\overline{5}$ V. 20.5 E. $13.708\overline{3}$ O. 64 M. 49.6 I. $5.1\overline{6}$

Mount Vesuvius

4·9 1. 32 2. 15.6 3. 27.1 4. 3.5 5. 31 6. 7.1 7. $19.\overline{3}$ 8. 5.025 9. $3.01\overline{6}$ 10. $5.8\overline{1}$ 11. 3.05 12. $2.9\overline{12}$ 13. $7.8\overline{1}$ 14. 1.6 15. 20.5 16. $31.3\overline{6}$

4·10 1. 7.25 2. 0.798 3. 3.18 4. 50 5. $11.8\overline{3}$ 6. 8.633 7. $8.\overline{3}$ 8. 3.2964 9. $17.\overline{7}$ 10. 6.556 11. 6.367 12. 0.2376 13. 0.404 14. 1.3 15. 3.528 16. 0.8375

5 Connecting fractions, decimals, and percents

5·1 1. 20% 2. 40% 3. 74% 4. 50% 5. 32% 6. 41% 7 to 12. Answers may vary. The percent indicates the number of squares that should be shaded.

5·2 D. 0.8 V. 0.36 I. 0.08 Y. 1 H. 0.015 L. 0.067 N. 15% O. 94% W. 150% E. 3.6% C. 9% T. 67%

wind velocity

5·3 1. 0.45 2. 0.75 3. 0.12 4. 0.058 5. 0.88 6. 0.912 7. 0.135 8. 1.2 9. 38% 10. 14% 11. 79% 12. 47.2% 13. 8.2% 14. 3% 15. 135% 16. 190%

5·4 A. 60% L. 62.5% D. 30% M. 90% H. 170% I. $33.\overline{3}$% Y. $36.\overline{36}$% S. 137.5% T. $166.\overline{6}$% N. $195.\overline{45}$%

Thailand . . . Siam

5·5 1. 70% 2. 20% 3. 87.5% 4. 22.$\overline{2}$% 5. 225% 6. 166.$\overline{6}$% 7. 175% 8. 91.$\overline{6}$% 9. 246.$\overline{6}$%
10. 40% 11. 16.$\overline{6}$% 12. 330% 13. 16% 14. 102% 15. 86.$\overline{6}$% 16. 355.$\overline{5}$%

5·6 O. $\frac{17}{100}$ M. $\frac{13}{25}$ P. $\frac{81}{200}$ S. $1\frac{1}{5}$ A. $\frac{9}{25}$ E. $\frac{1}{12}$ R. $1\frac{7}{20}$ H. $\frac{3}{4}$ N. $\frac{5}{6}$ I. $1\frac{19}{20}$
Roman Empire

5·7 1. $\frac{1}{10}$ 2. $\frac{1}{4}$ 3. $\frac{9}{20}$ 4. $\frac{119}{125}$ 5. $\frac{3}{100}$ 6. $1\frac{3}{4}$ 7. $\frac{97}{200}$ 8. $1\frac{3}{10}$ 9. $\frac{2}{3}$ 10. $\frac{1}{20}$ 11. $1\frac{1}{9}$ 12. $\frac{63}{100}$ 13. $1\frac{9}{10}$
14. $2\frac{489}{1000}$ 15. $\frac{83}{100}$ 16. $3\frac{13}{250}$

5·8 1. 0.25, 25% 2. $\frac{3}{4}$, 75% 3. 1, 1 4. $1\frac{3}{10}$, 130% 5. 0.8$\overline{3}$, 83.$\overline{3}$% 6. $\frac{39}{50}$, 0.78 7. 0.9, 90% 8. $\frac{3}{10}$,
30% 9. $1\frac{49}{100}$, 1.49 10. 0.02, 2% 11. $\frac{1}{100}$, 0.01 12. 0.625, 62.5% 13. $\frac{1}{11}$, 9.$\overline{09}$% 14. $\frac{7}{100}$,
0.07 15. 0.08$\overline{3}$, 8.$\overline{3}$% 16. $2\frac{2}{3}$, 2.$\overline{6}$

6 Operations with percents

6·1 O. 9 L. 50 T. 40 C. 150 A. 83.7 B. 16 I. 0.75 N. 1 K. 57.4 S. 20
abolitionist

6·2 1. 27 2. 15.64 3. 5 4. 16 5. 25 6. 45 7. 12 8. 30 9. 37.5 10. 170 11. 61.1 12. 31.25
13. 16 14. 2 15. 161.5 16. 11

6·3 U. 15 N. 1.5 I. 28 O. 22.5 V. 50% R. 75% H. 44% D. 13.$\overline{3}$% E. 46% S. 62.5%
Hudson River

6·4 1. 80% 2. 25% 3. 50% 4. 100% 5. 75% 6. 90% 7. 80% 8. 33.$\overline{3}$% 9. 83.$\overline{3}$% 10. 133.$\overline{3}$%
11. 66.$\overline{6}$% 12. 90% 13. 90% 14. 202% 15. 80% 16. 87.5%

6·5 A. 18 I. 50 E. 70 U. 15 T. 60 R. 75 B. 20 M. 42 H. 30 N. 120
Harriet Tubman

6·6 1. 50 2. 80 3. 35 4. 50 5. 30 6. 72 7. 200 8. 10 9. 70 10. 90 11. 49.5 12. 8 13. 20
14. 12 15. 144 16. 225

6·7 1. 5.25 2. 40 3. 100% 4. 82 5. 23.5 6. 50% 7. 56% 8. 4 9. 9 10. 83.$\overline{3}$% 11. 40%
12. 2% 13. 0.99 14. 9 15. 95 16. 12

6·8 A. $181.25 G. $18 O. 50% T. 62.5% F. $45 L. $1.75 I. 33.$\overline{3}$% N. 30% U. $3.58
S. $102.47 E. 6%
League of Nations

6·9 1. $26 2. 14% 3. 10% 4. $81.55 5. $54 6. 33.$\overline{3}$% 7. $25.12 8. 30% 9. $12.75 10. 5%
11. $48.75 12. 4%

6·10   L. 50%   U. 20%   A. 16.$\overline{6}$%   N. 33.$\overline{3}$%   E. 12.5%   C. 18.75%   S. 75%   P. 91.$\overline{6}$%   T. 25%
O. 48%

Cellulose . . . plants

6·11   1. 20%   2. 100%   3. 2.$\overline{2}$%   4. 10%   5. 8.$\overline{8}$%   6. 30%   7. 37.5%   8. 20%   9. 25%   10. 20%
11. 15%   12. 66.$\overline{6}$%   13. 51.$\overline{1}$%   14. 25%   15. 25%   16. 20%

6·12   M. $3,750   U. $550   E. $0.50   I. $6,000   P. 5   N. $75   T. $3,000   O. 5%   R. $2,750   C. 2.5%
D. 2   S. $2,500

compound interest

6·13   1. $160   2. $122.50   3. 10   4. 6%   5. $600   6. $196   7. 3   8. $3,125   9. 4   10. 8%   11. 4
12. $192.50   13. $575   14. 3.9%   15. $2,730   16. $200,000